HOW THEY DREW IT UP

BAYLOR'S UNFORGETTABLE 2021 CHAMPIONSHIP SEASON

SBNATION
OUR DAILY BEARS

2021 NC
INDIANA. WHE
GONZAGA
CREIGHTON
USC
OREGO
GONZA
BAYLOR BEARS
CHAMPS
FINAL FOUR
NCAA.COM/FIN
ATIONAL CH

This book is available in quantity at special discounts for your group or organization. For further information, contact:

Triumph Books LLC
814 North Franklin Street
Chicago, Illinois 60610
Phone: (312) 337-0747
www.triumphbooks.com

Printed in U.S.A.
ISBN: 978-1-62937-941-8

Content packaged by Mojo Media, Inc.
Joe Funk: Editor
Jason Hinman: Creative Director

Front and back cover photos by AP Images

Except where otherwise noted, all interior photos by AP Images.

CONTENTS

FOREWORD

By Scott Drew

We like to use the term J.O.Y. It means you play for Jesus first, then Others, then finally Yourself. That's not an easy thing to do in today's world, but it's the motto this team had. And it's the way they lived out that motto that explains why I think—for as good of players as we had, they were even better people.

With the bubble, we all got to spend a lot of time together in Indianapolis. The great thing about that is how much we enjoyed each other's company. We played Connect Four and corn hole to pass the time. Some of the games got as competitive as the basketball games. Some of our guys still argue about how those games in the bubble went down.

This was a special group of players and coaches. After COVID-19 ended last season, they came back focused on firsts. They wanted to be the first team to go undefeated at the Ferrell Center. They did that. They wanted to be the first Baylor team to win a Big 12 championship. They did that. They wanted to be the first Baylor team since 1950 to make the Final Four. They did that. And they wanted to be the first Baylor team to win a national title. They did that.

Winning in college basketball isn't easy. I've been on the right side of some of the biggest moments in the NCAA Tournament and on some of the toughest ones too. If you coach college basketball for very long, then everyone has those kinds of moments.

We were blessed to have such great players that gave us a chance to compete and win a national title. They dealt with a COVID-19 pause where multiple players were not just in quarantine but had the virus. We weren't quite the same team immediately after we returned, but they continued to believe we could get back to that level. Another amazing thing about our team though was the effort and accountability from our players, coaches and staff. They had big goals and they achieved all of them. They didn't let an excuse stop them from achieving their goals.

I'm proud and humbled by all we achieved this season. We couldn't have done it without the support of our athletic director, Mack Rhoades, and our president Linda Livingstone. The assistant coaches, graduate assistants, managers and athletics administration worked relentlessly to make all this happen too. And we're so thankful to the NCAA for all of their effort to make sure we got to experience March Madness.

Our team achieved so much because of the players. They're the most important part and anyone that's followed college basketball knows that. These

Scott Drew accepted the Baylor coaching position in 2003, at a time few others wanted it. Now, the Baylor Bears are national champions.

men believed in our vision. They provided servant leadership by sometimes sacrificing their own role for a better chance to win games. That's not easy to do, and we wouldn't have achieved all that we did without the buy-in from our players.

Kendall covered the team all season. He was there every single time we met with the media, and he always asked detailed questions about analytics and lineups throughout our press conferences. He

profiled many of our players and provided new information about the things they overcame and used to become champions. We're grateful for his dedication to covering of our team. We hope you have as much fun reading this detailed book about our team as we had playing.

To all of the Baylor Family, thank you so much for your support and faith in us. We couldn't have done it without you! ∎

INTRODUCTION

This should never have happened at Baylor University. The disadvantages Baylor faces: smaller alumni base, no basketball history and a powerhouse basketball program in its own league, should have made what ended on April 5th in Indianapolis impossible.

Scott Drew took over the Baylor University job in 2003. Coming off a scandal where one player murdered another, Drew embraced building a program with almost no history to fall back on. From 1951 to 2003, Baylor made one NCAA Tournament. Located in the heart of Texas, most people at Baylor only cared about football.

Drew saw something at Baylor. I graduated from Baylor, so I understand the appeal of the university. Baylor has real advantages. It's a strong academic institution and one of the only Christian universities in a power five conference. Texas has some of the country's best high school players.

Even with those advantages, going from good to great remained a monumental task. Baylor made the Elite Eight in 2010 and 2012. But going from the end of the second weekend to winning the final weekend is difficult. Multiple men are in the College Basketball Hall of Fame without a Final Four.

During the 2019-2020 season, Baylor had the best team in program history. The Bears won a Big 12 record 23 consecutive games. Jared Butler told me that the team felt unbeatable during that run. Even with a 2-3 slide to end the regular season,

the Bears thought they were going to win the 2019-2020 NCAA Tournament. But COVID struck, and the NCAA elected to cancel the tournament. Suddenly the best Baylor team ever just had to argue what might have been.

That summer, Baylor had four major NBA decisions. Mark Vital announced in late April that he'd come back. Vital felt like he had to win a national title.

Jared Butler, Davion Mitchell and MaCio Teague all came back too. Mitchell told me that he wanted to improve his offense. After shooting 45% from deep on the year, he should be a lottery pick.

Teague and Butler went through the draft process, and each seriously thought about going pro. Both told me there were days they thought they would not return to Baylor. Each had unique reasons for coming back. Yet the allure of winning a title at Baylor brought them back.

This book chronicles the many ups and few downs of the best season in Baylor history. There's a good argument this is the best team in Big 12 history. The 2008 Jayhawks are the only other Big 12 team to win a national title. Those Jayhawks had worse losses and needed Mario Chalmers' miracle to beat Memphis.

The Bears needed no miracles on their run to a national title. After a COVID pause put them in a difficult spot—nearly losing to Iowa State and getting handled easily by Kansas—the Bears responded. They had difficult film sessions and

Davion Mitchell takes a moment to sit with the trophy following Baylor's win over Gonzaga in the national championship game.

practices. With so much time together, they could hold each other accountable.

During the NCAA Tournament, Baylor proved its dominance. Only one team kept it within single digits and nine points isn't exactly close.

The win over Gonzaga might be the most impressive win of all-time. Basketball's history is too long that some will chide that statement to recency bias. I just know that I was in the arena for that one, and nobody in college basketball history would have eviscerated Gonzaga like that.

The Bulldogs entered No. 1 in the country. Two days before the game, I texted Rem Bakamus, a graduate assistant and former player at Gonzaga. He felt confident that Baylor would win this game. He knew well how good Gonzaga was, but after a year of working with the team, he knew Baylor had another tier. It showed that on the final night of the season.

The Gonzaga game required Baylor's coaching staff to go to work. I got a call from one Baylor assistant while I tried to power through spaghetti at a Buca di Beppo. While people walked in and out of the restaurant, I earnestly listened while he described the plan. Baylor would front All-American Drew Timme and hope to turn him over. They'd also hunt mismatches and make sure the guards got him in plenty of screens. Both those things worked to perfection.

This was an unusual team in so many ways. Located in Texas, Baylor had just one rotation player from the state. Jerome Tang, the lead assistant, is the most overqualified man for that position in sports. John Jakus is one of the best offensive minds around and worked the scout for the Gonzaga victory. Al Brooks coached against his father—also named Al Brooks—and scouted the Cougars so well that Kelvin Sampson would say after the game that the 2020-2021 Bears were the best team he'd ever coached against in his seven years there.

It was the honor of a lifetime to cover this team. I watched plenty of them grow personally and professionally. Interviews that should have lasted 30- or 45-minutes dragged on. In late February, I told David Kaye—Baylor's exceptional SID—that I wanted 30 minutes with Butler. After 45 minutes, Butler asked me plenty of questions about my own life. When I wasn't feeling great personally, he helped me out. That embodied Baylor's mantra—Jesus, Others, Yourself—that Scott Drew wrote about in the foreword.

This could have ended poorly. After spending several hours interviewing every major rotation piece and plenty of hours with coaches and assistants, I dreaded the possibility I'd have to write that final story explaining why they came up just short.

They never made me do that. Instead, the Bears cut down the nets on Tuesday morning in Indianapolis. They hugged and cried, laughed and shouted. They came here with hope and left as champions.

It was the honor of a lifetime to cover this team, and I hope the stories that follow give some insight into the biggest moments and players on that run. ■

— *Kendall Kaut*

Eighteen years after taking over a men's basketball program in shambles, head coach Scott Drew lifts the championship trophy.

Baylor 78, Houston 59

April 3, 2021 ▪ **Indianapolis, Indiana**

A DATE WITH DESTINY

Baylor Played Like a National Champion in Win Over Houston

Jared Butler steps up and drains the three. Then Davion Mitchell takes a giant step to his left to swish another three before halftime ends. Twenty minutes of game time have elapsed in Lucas Oil Stadium, and Houston must realize its season will end in the next 20 minutes of play. Baylor heads into the locker room up 45-20, and sure enough, the Bears handle Houston in the second half to emerge 78-59.

For the first time since 1948, Baylor is playing for a men's national championship. Black men could not attend, much less play for Baylor then. This collection of men overwhelms opponents. After the game, Kelvin Sampson said, "But so impressed with Baylor. I keep going back to them— Butler, Mitchell, Teague, Flagler, Mayer. I don't think I've seen a team with five guards at that level. No drop off. And they're good at both ends."

Baylor is more than its two-headed monster of Mitchell and Butler, but the pair is quite the monster to take on. Mitchell finished with 11 assists and no turnovers. Butler added 17 first-half points and went 4-of-5 from deep. He exploited Houston's pick-and-roll decisions. "We did a good job understanding what they were doing," he explained following the win. "We got in the groove of what they were doing, and we were able to take advantage of it."

You could go on-and-on about Baylor's play. Jonathan Tchamwa Tchatchoua hit a floater en route to 11 points. Matthew Mayer made threes. Adam Flagler contested shots, and MaCio Teague moved the ball well.

Then there's the defense. Baylor held Houston to just .645 points per possession in the first half. Most years, the nation's worst offense scores .87 points per possession, and Houston—a Final Four participant—sure isn't the nation's worst offense. Outside of Marcus Sassar, Houston scored just three points in the first half. If he hadn't gotten it going with some difficult looks, Houston might have been the victim of the worst Final Four loss ever.

Houston made a bit of a run in the second half. The Cougars got within 20 points, but then—as always seems to be the case—Baylor responded. Tchamwa Tchatchoua got open in the middle of the court on pick-and-rolls. Houston tried to adjust, but Baylor's adjustments were simply too much.

When asked about the Bears' defense after the game, Scott Drew credited the work of assistant

Baylor and Davion Mitchell cruised against the Cougars in the Lone Star State battle, winning 78-59. Mitchell had 12 points and 11 assists in the comfortable win.

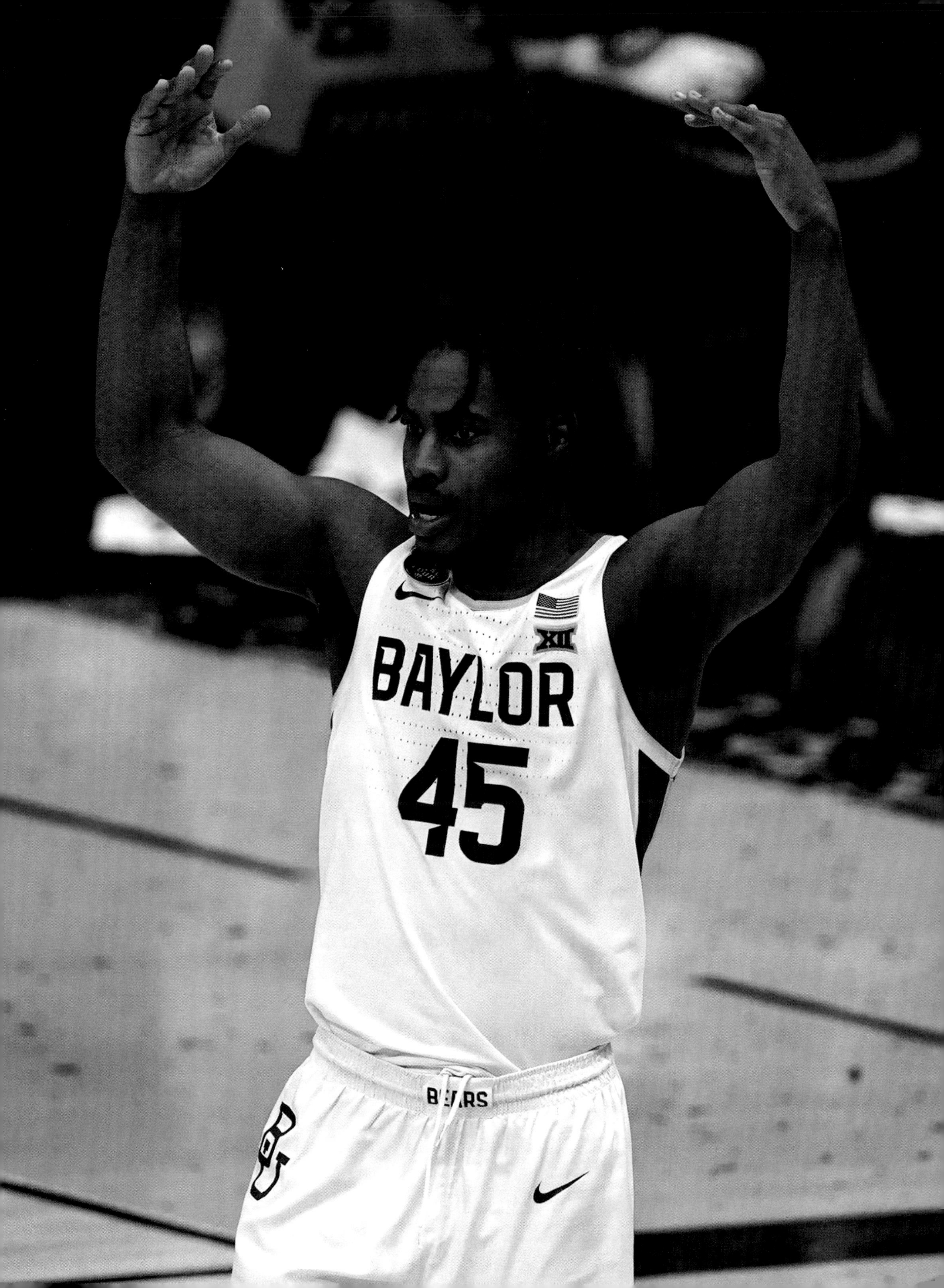
BAYLOR
45
BEARS

Baylor guard Jared Butler (12) passes over teammate Adam Flagler (10) and Houston forward Justin Gorham (4) during the first half of the dominant win. Butler had 17 points, five rebounds and four assists.

coach Alvin Brooks III. "Coach Brooks did a great job on the scout. I think we were prepared. And really our guys did a great job buying into—locking in on assignments and tendencies."

The Final Four match-up saw Brooks coaching against his father, Houston assistant Alvin Brooks Jr. This win marked the first time the son had defeated the father.

The Bears won so convincingly that Sampson said, "That's the best team that I've seen in the seven years I've been at Houston. They're really, really good."

The standard for Baylor all season has been Gonzaga. And for Gonzaga, it's been Baylor. While each team will say publicly that they focus on themselves and going 1-0 each day, the cliches can't mask the reality that each has been waiting for the other.

Now Baylor will get that opportunity. The Bears won't score 1.34 points per possession most nights or have everyone playing at such an exemplary level across the board. But they don't need that to win the title. Still, the fact that Baylor can provides more evidence it can absolutely beat Gonzaga. ∎

Baylor forward Flo Thamba (0) grabs a rebound, one of his four in the Final Four victory over Houston.

The Baylor Bears were all smiles at the end of a lopsided win over Houston, which set up a showdown with the undefeated Gonzaga Bulldogs in the championship game.

Baylor 86, Gonzaga 70
April 5, 2021 ▪ Indianapolis, Indiana

THE UNSTOPPABLE TITLE PATH

Baylor Slays Undefeated Gonzaga to Win Program's First National Title

After Gonzaga entered this game undefeated and as the highest ranked team in the 19 years of KenPom's data, Baylor eviscerated Gonzaga 86-70 to win the program's first title.

Baylor felt like it could do this. The programs were set to meet on December 5, 2020. After that game was canceled, I had a then-off-the-record discussion with John Jakus, an assistant coach. He coached at Gonzaga, and we spent 10 minutes discussing it.

Jakus noted that the relationship between the programs is deeper than anyone really contemplates. He said, "I talk to people from there every day." He added, "People don't understand just how connected Scott and Mark are. Their friendship is so real, and they're so close."

With that immense respect, Jakus highlighted that Gonzaga was the best passing team since at the least the 2015 Duke team that won a national title. He felt like too many teams played Gonzaga conservatively. While that idea made some sense — Gonzaga was the country's top 2-point shooting team and few teams have the pieces to handle Jalen Suggs, Corey Kispert and Drew Timme —Jakus was adamant that opponents had to pressure Gonzaga to have a chance to win.

Jakus told me, "Most teams don't have the personnel to try it, but nobody had really tried it." So the Bears elected to pressure the ball and make every pass difficult. Maybe Gonzaga would take advantage of that pressure with too many fouls. That happened some, but the Bears won the tradeoff. Gonzaga looked a step slower than Baylor's defense.

The Bears came out fronting Drew Timme, which left a player in front of him and made passing to him difficult. Once he caught the ball, he didn't have the usual freedom that led to him scoring 100 combined points in his previous four NCAA Tournament games. He would finish this night with just 12 points.

After the game, Mark Few said, "They were just so much more aggressive. They literally — we haven't played like that this year. They literally busted us out of anything we could possibly do on offense. We were playing with our back to the basket — not facing up. And we couldn't get anything generated to the basket; we were kind of playing sideways."

That Baylor strategy — make passing difficult — ruined so many of Gonzaga's sets. The Bulldogs finished with just 1.03 adjusted points per possession — their lowest mark of the season. After the game, Scott Drew said, "We're really good defensively. I thought we made things tough tonight. Gonzaga missed some shots that they probably normally make. But credit our guys for

Jonathan Tchamwa Tchatchoua dunks the ball against Gonzaga during the second half. The Bears built up a comfortable lead by halftime and continued their aggressive approach until the final buzzer.

making everything difficult. Coach Jakus was on their staff there and is obviously familiar with the program. He had a great scouting report. Credit the players then for executing it."

Both Drew and Jakus would credit the players first, and I'm sure Jakus would prefer I mention him later in this story. But plenty of other writers have written about how Baylor's players powered them to the victory. That's important; but it took Baylor deciding that it would play an aggressive defense that few others would try to win this game.

Once again, Baylor raced out to a giant lead. The Bears led 9-0 and then 35-16. But over the final five minutes, Gonzaga went with a zone and cut the Baylor lead to 10 points. During halftime, the mood felt a bit uneasy. Gonzaga trailed BYU at halftime of the WCC Tournament, then raced back to win by double digits. On the sport's biggest stage, Baylor had to answer.

As they had so often this season, Baylor responded. Jared Butler opened the second half with back-to-back threes. Gonzaga's zone — a scheme they probably never planned to play much against the country's top 3-point shooting team — left an opening at the top. Butler just took that opening and fired early in the shot clock. Few noted after the game, "They hit back-to-back 3s on it. So they scored six straight points. And then tried it one more time and they got either a high-post jumper or a guy caught it in the middle of the zone and bounced down. So they scored eight quick points against it."

Baylor showed it could win in so many ways tonight. Jonathan Tchamwa Tchatchoua played aggressive defense that kept the ball on the side. Jakus told me, "We knew we wanted to have him late." But he picked up his third foul in the first half. The Baylor staff debated reinserting him, and once he picked up his third foul, it was easy to

MaCio Teague shoots over Gonzaga forwards Drew Timme and Corey Kispert during the first half. Teague scored 19 points against the Bulldogs.

second guess the decision. The Bears had played aggressively all year though, confident if something went wrong, a backup plan could carry them.

That backup plan worked as Mark Vital played long stretches at the five. I dubbed those lineups the Fival — Vital at the five, after the old children's movie. Vital told me, "I like that nickname. If you like it, I love it." With his speed, Baylor corralled offensive rebounds and got out to shooters quickly. Gonzaga's offense — the nation's No. 1 rated attack — suddenly looked creaky. If not for Suggs making a few plays late, this might have ended with Gonzaga losing by more than 20.

The Bears simply had too many guys for Gonzaga. Matthew Mayer drew plenty of attention, allowing the Baylor guards to get open. Adam Flagler swept across the lane for an offensive rebound, one of 16 on the day for Baylor. The Bears grabbed 49 percent of their missed shots, an outrageous number that contributed to so many deflating sequences for Gonzaga. Multiple times it felt like Gonzaga played decent defense against a well-moving Baylor offense. Then Baylor, led by Vital's eight offensive boards, got another chance and drained a three.

Few teams in the history of the sport could have beaten Baylor tonight. The Bears shot 10-of-23 from three and made 16 of 18 free throws. They had just nine turnovers too. The Bears scored so effectively that Gonzaga tried switching and going under. Zone and man-to-man. Doubling and token pressure. None of those options worked. Nothing would have tonight.

The win should put Baylor into the discussion for the greatest team of all-time. Baylor entered the NCAA Tournament as the No. 2 overall seed. Baylor did that despite missing 19 days with a COVID infection. Jakus stressed that the COVID situation — with the restrictions for the players

Jared Butler led Baylor's offensive effort with 22 points in the championship game, matching Gonzaga star Jalen Suggs.

and the virus sweeping across the team — made this a more difficult season than those outside could grasp. From talks with players, multiple guys on the team contracted it. Jeff Goodman of Stadium reported eight Baylor players had it. I can confirm that the virus ravaged the team during that stretch and hit about everyone. Several had rough stretches.

Even without minimizing the COVID pause and Baylor's loss to Kansas, Baylor tore through this tournament. Davion Mitchell won all three defensive player of the year awards. He made Suggs' life difficult, and probably should have drawn a third foul on Gonzaga's point guard when Suggs grew so frustrated he threw Mitchell out of bounds reaching for a loose ball along the sidelines.

Nobody should underestimate how impressive what Baylor did to Gonzaga is. Gonzaga played just two single-digit games all season — a win over West Virginia and a Final Four win over UCLA. The Bulldogs blew out Kansas, Virginia, Iowa, Oklahoma, Creighton and USC. They made potential top five draft picks look like high school players. Vegas thought the Bulldogs were 4.5 points better than the Bears. Reality had something else to say.

MaCio Teague and Adam Flagler combined for 32 points. The third and fourth best guards on the team both shot over 40 percent from three on the season. That any team would have that pair as its third and fourth best guards is ridiculous.

After a long season — with a 30-day bubble in a downtown Marriott — Baylor celebrated its national title. The men embraced and rushed for t-shirts that declared themselves champions. Drew high-fived with fans and Teague signed autographs. They'd earned all of this and achieved it. ■

All smiles, the full Baylor Bears squad of players and coaches celebrates with the trophy after the championship game.

REACHING THE APEX

Jared Butler Does it All in Winning a Championship, Most Outstanding Player Award

After starting 6-of-24 from deep in the NCAA Tournament, Jared Butler finished with 20 points and seven assists to knock off Gonzaga to win the national title and Most Outstanding Player of the Final Four. He went 8-of-14 from deep in the Final Four and title game.

About an hour after Baylor's players passed around the trophy and exchanged hugs and laughs, Butler stepped to the computer to Zoom (how sad has the last year been that Zoom can become a verb?) with the media. With his trademark charisma, he shouted, "Aye, Kendall, my guy."

I've written about Butler for the last three years. We've had plenty of long conversations about basketball and life, politics and dating. But mostly, it's about what few people that have ever lived can play better than him: basketball.

Gonzaga pushed Baylor to end the first half. With Jonathan Tchamwa Tchatchoua, Flo Thamba and Mark Vital combining for eight fouls, the Bulldogs cut a 19-point first half deficit to 10. As the highest rated KenPom team of all-time, plenty of Baylor fans felt nervous at the prospect of matching the seemingly inevitable Gonzaga run.

I talked with seven Baylor fans as I waited to buy water during halftime. All felt a bit uneasy. The anxiety of trying to win the first national title in program history made all of them afraid the night would end with stories about Baylor blowing a 19-point lead.

Butler opened the second half draining two triples. The Bulldogs' hope that they could zone Baylor—the nation's top 3-point shooting team—died a quick death as his form and ability proved too much. Two years ago, back when he was barely an adult, he told me, "I've never really had to work on my form. I've been blessed that way."

There are few folks smarter and more gracious than Butler. I've spent hours talking X's and O's with him. During quarantine I screen shared my computer and we broke down play after play. He talked about getting better on defense and how he changed the way he watched film. I talked with graduate assistants that mentioned he'd started working like a professional. He'd get in and out for workouts without wasting a minute. He was generous with his time but exacting to make sure he didn't waste the time of others.

That framework came to fruition as Butler often kept Jalen Suggs from getting into the paint. He worked well to keep the ball on the side, and when Corey Kispert—a likely lottery pick—ended up on his side of the floor, Butler stopped his 3-point opportunities.

After three great years of knowing him, Butler and I have discussed X's and O's enough. I got the chance to ask him what it means to be the MOP and a national champion. He told me, "Man, I'm not trying to preach a prosperity gospel, but our Lord and Savior, I say it all the time: He gets us through everything. Jesus Christ, man, he's the truth. And he was with us tonight. He was with us all season. He was with us wherever we go."

Some will scoff at that. There are plenty of atheists when their team loses a basketball game. But there's no doubt in the best moment of his life, Butler believed something higher explained the apex of his life. And with the way he played tonight, he'll have plenty of teams clamoring to select him in the 2021 NBA Draft. ∎

Jared Butler withdrew from the 2020 NBA Draft to return to Baylor, citing "unfinished business." Butler was named the Final Four Most Outstanding Player after his team's dominant 86–70 win over Gonzaga for the national title.

ROAD TO THE TITLE

THE BEST BAYLOR TEAM EVER AND THE ETERNAL WHAT IF

Fans Will Always Wonder What Would Have Happened in March 2020

March 12, 2020

They had the nation's longest streak at No. 1 since 2015. Their 23 straight wins were the most of the 270 Big 12 teams that played a full season in the league. But because of a global pandemic, we'll never know exactly how the 2019-2020 Bears would have done in March.

This was a special team. Despite featuring zero top 30 consensus recruits, the roster was loaded with talent. The best players in America are often freshman. Sometimes it's better to be a little older though, and Baylor proved that. They didn't play any freshman. And four of the five starters redshirted.

The team's best player was Jared Butler. He was a unanimous selection to the first team in the Big 12. He earned All-American honors from multiple outlets. When the Bears needed a bucket, he was a steadying force. He dropped 22 points in Allen Fieldhouse, earning Baylor the program's first win in that building and leading Baylor to a 12-point win. The Jayhawks didn't lose another game after that, and their two previous losses were by a combined three points.

Several guys have a legitimate case for being the team's next best player, and that's where the strength of the team resonated. Freddie Gillespie went from Division III to a scholarship player at Baylor. Out of the rotation late in his junior season, he entered the rotation because of an injury to Tristan Clark and became All-Big 12 Second Team and a member of the defensive team. His ability to switch pick-and-rolls and block shots helped Baylor switch to a no middle defense. That defense finished 4th on KenPom, which is 19 spots higher than any previous Baylor team.

Davion Mitchell was a maniac on defense. Nobody could defend on the ball like him. In Ames, he took flight with one of the most impressive blocks you'll ever see. With him hounding opposing guards, Baylor's defense went from No. 85 in defensive efficiency in 2019 to 4th in 2020.

MaCio Teague came from UNC-Ashville and established himself as a reliable isolation scorer. If there was a flaw to Baylor's season it's that the offense could sometimes bog down. But Teague was a wizard finding late scoring opportunities. Against Texas Tech, his stepback three ended the Red Raiders in Waco.

Mark Vital was named the captain of Seth Davis' all glue team, a fitting honor for America's most underrated player. Vital could truly defend every position on the court. Baylor's twitter account had a clip from every game about, "Going Vital," and those clips were as reliable every week as the joy the team brought to the fans.

The bench helped the team immensely. Devonte Bandoo was the microwave and conference's best sixth man. He was never afraid to pull from anywhere, and didn't sulk that he played way less at Baylor than he would have somewhere else. He just made shots when it mattered.

Matt Mayer may have ended the inevitable trajectory of every white basketball player needing

A former walk-on transfer, Freddie Gillespie started all 30 games for Baylor during the 2019-2020 season. Gillespie's career at Baylor came to an abrupt end with the cancelation of the 2020 postseason.

another white basketball comparison. His game and career have followed Taurean Prince's. Once a man as prone to moments of catastrophe as moments of jubilation, he threw down a dunk on West Virginia that was Jordanesque.

Tristan Clark battled through knee issues after missing half of last season. He seemed thrilled to play in the NCAA Tournament, and he displayed his skilled back to the basket game against Oklahoma. Clark still hasn't gotten the chance to play in the NCAA Tournament while at Baylor, a reminder of how cruel life can be.

Flo Thamba provided needed depth and stayed ready, even as he wasn't always in the rotation. Those kind of guys can kill a squad if they overreact to their limited minutes. Instead, he came in and provided quality defense.

The 2020 Bears were a testament to a coaching staff that was willing to change everything to become better than ever. Scott Drew completed the greatest turnaround in college basketball history when he took Baylor to the 2010 Elite Eight after the lows the program went through under Dave Bliss. He built a solid run over the rest of the decade by primarily playing zone defense. Often the Bears ran out talented freshmen like Perry Jones, Quincy Miller and Isaiah Austin.

The 2020 Bears decided to change things. They switched to that no middle defense, which hounded opponent after opponent. He worked different lineups, turning to four guards and a big man. They sometimes played Vital at center. They gave Mayer major minutes at the four. They knew to be the best team in program history they had to be a little different, and that's so incredibly difficult. When things are going pretty great it's hard to make a change so things can just be great. Drew and his staff did that and things were real and spectacular.

The future is unknowable. Nobody previewing the 2020 basketball season predicted, "We won't even play the NCAA Tournament because someone

Big 12 commissioner Bob Bowlsby is seen on the big screen at Kansas City's Sprint Center as he announces the cancelation of the remaining 2020 Big 12 Conference tournament games.

will eat a bat in China that will cause a global pandemic." It's still baffling to think Baylor's season didn't end with them playing basketball.

We know that Baylor fans will always say they could have won the NCAA Tournament. Yes, Baylor went 2-3 down the stretch. They lost by three to Kansas, who would have joined Baylor as a No. 1 seed. The Bears fell to TCU with Vital injured. They lost to West Virginia in Morgantown with the following players injured: Clark (out), Vital (hobbled), Mayer (didn't play the second half), Bandoo (missed much of the game) and Teague (wrist). The Bears felt they were finally healthy again for the Big 12 and NCAA Tournament. The team that had won 23 straight games and still had a No. 1 seed secured thought they were back. And that team — the one that beat Villanova, Butler and Arizona — was ready to eviscerate a sport that listed them at 500-1 odds before the season to win a national championship.

The Bears really could have won the title. And not in a, "2014 Connecticut won the title" way. They were legitimately one of the country's best teams and could have done it. Sometime in the next 50 years, there will be great Baylor teams. Hopefully there will be many. But whenever there's a great team, this year's team will be the standard they'll measure themselves against. They'll wonder if they have a scorer like Butler. A worker and defender like Gillespie. A guard that can end another guards' offense like Mitchell. A sixth man like Bandoo. Someone that can reliably get a bucket like Teague. And a man who can guard anyone on any court like Vital.

In February, Gillespie told me, "Everyone has an expiration date that plays the game." That quote stuck with me today. Much like this Baylor team will for years. For as long as I live, I'll wonder what if they'd had a chance in the NCAA Tournament? This team deserved an answer to that question, but it's pretty special they were good enough to make us all wonder. ∎

Devonte Bandoo arrived at Baylor in 2018 via transfer from Hutchinson Community College in Kansas and developed into the Big 12's top sixth man his senior season. Bandoo's career was cut short with the cancelation of the 2020 postseason.

12
GUARD

JARED BUTLER
All-American Explains Why He Returned to Baylor
August 14, 2020

In the 113-year history of Baylor basketball, the program has never opened a season ranked higher than No. 12. But with Jared Butler back, the Bears begin the season No. 1 on ESPN's 2020-2021 rankings.

Butler spoke with me about his sophomore campaign, the NBA Draft process and his decision to return to Baylor.

To understand how Butler came to his decision and understand his game, it's helpful to look back at his rise.

Before COVID-19 would preclude American entry in Europe, the 2019-2020 Bears played a four-game series in Italy. And that trip changed the tenor for the team. Butler said, "It was a great experience for individuals living in the U.S. to get to go outside of the country. Italy was amazing; as the team, it really helped us bond a lot. (We) spent 10 days in a foreign country with so many things to do. Playing there was really helpful."

Their strong performance in Italy led plenty of us to hype last season's squad. But the Bears blew a double-digit lead to Washington in early November. MaCio Teague told me that, "Jared might have been the only person that played well." Butler noted the loss was "probably the best thing that happened to us. It humbled us a lot. Put us on track to where we needed to be and took us down from cloud nine."

In the Myrtle Beach Invitational, Villanova and Baylor may have played the most enjoyable game of the season. Both teams shot over 50% from the field. The Bears made 57% of their 3-point attempts. Butler finished with 22 points to lead Baylor to the victory. Butler said, "We were great. Villanova was great. It comes down to who is going to be the tougher team. Who will get a stop on defense. We all knew: who gets a stop?" Baylor managed to hold off the Wildcats and continue a winning streak that would top out at 23 games; the longest in the 24-year history of the Big 12.

To the chagrin of Baylor's basketball fans, Allen Fieldhouse had been where Baylor's best teams go to lose. The Bears had led at halftime and fallen. They'd had solid leads with two minutes remaining and perished. And they had plenty of instances where they experienced what one of the 20th Century's great thinkers, Viktor Frankl, called "Delusions of Reprieve," which is a belief just

Jared Butler was Baylor's leading scorer in 2020-2021, averaging 16.5 points per game while shooting over 46 percent from the floor.

before someone is doomed that things are about to actually turn in their favor. But whether it was a call that didn't get made, or Baylor didn't make that one final stop or the Bears didn't hit one big shot, Baylor went into Kansas' arena 14 times and left with 14 losses. That's understandable. Kansas has been one of the country's premiere programs. Buddy Hield dropped 46 points while playing for the country's top ranked team and walked out of Allen Fieldhouse a loser. Kevin Durant scored 25 points in the first half there, and still, Texas lost too.

History remains constant until it doesn't. And on January 11, 2020, Butler excised the mentality that haunted Baylor's past forays in Lawrence, Kansas. Despite dropping 31 points in Allen Fieldhouse in 2019, the Bears lost. Butler said, "The year before, just going into Allen Fieldhouse, everybody on the team didn't believe we could win. That was really hard for me."

Butler took control and changed things. He said, "With a whole new group of guys, they didn't have the monkey of years on their back. They didn't know how much weight it was. We as competitors looked at someone just as good as us, and we wanted to prove our work was better."

Purists often argue about slippery slopes. If we don't maintain a narrow view of what's allowed, then someday — though maybe not immediately — we'll regret how someone manipulates the new strictures.

In the NBA, James Harden has pushed the limits of what's considered a gather to get more steps than a dieter on the first week with a Fitbit. Butler has done the same thing to the rules about what's a carry. As college basketball and the NBA allowed players to progressively get away with their wrist closer to the ground than the ceiling while dribbling, a skilled player, like Butler, can now make it nearly impossible for a defender to understand when a player has picked up their dribble.

At the end of the first half, Christian Braun learned how impossible it is to defend Butler. Braun ended up fouling him because he couldn't be certain if Butler was ready to shoot or still had a path to the basket. When Braun opened his hips, he gave Butler a split second to get to the hoop and draw the foul.

In the second half, Butler showed why Braun wasn't crazy for thinking Butler would shoot in the first half. Butler said, "This was the moment when I got back in the game. I was like, 'it's a little too close for me.' I think I hit one shot and okay, let's go. Coach Drew ran some plays. It was just too close. I didn't want the refs to get involved. I didn't want outside factors, and I knew it was a big moment."

Marcus Garrett won the Naismith Defensive Player of the Year, which is given to the country's best defender. He can defend any position, and in Morgantown, his efforts over the final eight minutes sent top 25 West Virginia's season spiraling. But Butler was a little too good for him. Butler said, "He definitely is one of the best defenders. My will was a little bit more. I had scored a bunch before this. I had a lot more confidence and this mode where I was going to get a bucket for our team."

Perhaps Baylor's toughest loss in Allen Fieldhouse came in 2017. That Baylor team would also achieve a No. 1 ranking during the regular season. But they committed a catastrophic error late in the game. Al Freeman went under a screen against Frank Mason, and Baylor lost.

History rhymed in Baylor's favor thanks to Butler. Garrett committed a mistake similar to Freeman's. Garrett went under and gave Baylor a chance to end the game. Butler said, "I did pause for a second. It was more of wow. But just kind of like, they were just getting confused on how to guard it.

Trying to find a different way to stop it. This is the easiest bucket of all the buckets I've had."

The Jayhawks returned to Waco for one of the most hyped games in Big 12 regular season history. Baylor broke Kansas' streak for the most consecutive wins in Big 12 history. The Jayhawks hadn't lost to anyone since the Baylor game. The two squads would make up 20% of the All-American teams and 100% of the league's all-defensive unit.

After a run late, Baylor had the ball down three. They worked a play for Butler, and his shot just missed. He said, "My mindset is to try and get the best shot off. Just left it short by like four inches, or I would have made the shot. I felt like I had a great shot and could have had it. That's a 2-of-4 shot if I did it again."

That was a brutally tough loss for Baylor. They finished 15-3, but were denied a league crown. No team had ever won 15 games and failed to win the league title.

The world deserved to see those teams play in the Big 12 Tournament and the Final Four. Butler, adept at analyzing how things might have changed in those games said, "We would have adjusted to their middle ball screen. We would have had a different plan. It would have been a mindset. The first game, we destroyed them. The second game, they destroyed us on offense. It would have been a mind match. Everyone knowing everyone's moves. It would have been a tremendous game. I can't say for sure what would have happened."

In a hotel ballroom in Kansas City, Baylor officially found out the NCAA Tournament was cancelled because of COVID-19. That left plenty of players with NBA Draft decisions.

Baylor could have lost four guys to the NBA Draft. Davion Mitchell, the team's point guard, told me in January about the possibility he'd leave

early, "I really don't know the future." Mark Vital, the team's starting power forward, told me, "It took me a month to decide what to do." And Teague, Baylor's other starting guard went through the NBA Draft process and told me last month that he made the decision to come back only two weeks before the NBA Draft deadline.

With the uncertainty about if any of those guys would come back, Butler entered the NBA Draft. He said that he interviewed with 23 NBA teams over Zoom. He explained, "All of the interviews were similar and group meetings and a guy asking questions and listening. Some distinct features. Some would ask me to break down film and hear thoughts. Some had different psychological evaluations and things with them. Some were personal and interrogative."

The NBA also likes to give out mental tests. That makes sense to some degree. When NBA teams couldn't get players in live contact drills because of local ordinances restricting travel and gatherings, they could find out someone's mental acuity and personality. But sometimes things go too far. Butler told me he took the Myers-Briggs personality test. That tests asks people what they'd prefer between two options. Then people are scored on four different categories. Study after study finds the test has no scientific value. Scrolling through Facebook posts from 2012 or texting an ex is a better use of anyone's time than taking that test. Butler offered no complaint about being subjected to that grave injustice. Maybe that suggests he has the demeanor to thrive in every locker oom. Or maybe it suggests even the NBA couldn't escape the bastion of stupidity that is the Myers-Briggs test.

Butler had an inquisitive mindset during the process. He asked teams pointed questions to ensure they provided him the best intelligence about if

returning to school or going pro was his best option. He said that the NBA teams liked, "My ability to play with and without the ball. They felt in their system they could plug me in different situations and be comfortable with my role." He also learned what the NBA wanted him to improve on. He said there were "Three things. Athleticism, being able to improve assist to turnover and my defense. I can get better on defense guarding the ball."

He told me there were several times he leaned toward staying in the NBA Draft, "Many different times. Especially when you're training as a professional and the lifestyle you start to enjoy and stay comfortable with staying in the draft. There were times I thought the opposite too. I was leaning one way at times."

Ultimately, Butler had to balance two things. First, he said, "When it came down to the last few weeks, the big consensus to be a first round draft pick and the chance of me being a first round pick were much slimmer." He felt like he was going to be drafted somewhere in the second round. Second, Butler also had to consider what Baylor had coming back. By the time he made his decision, he knew Baylor had 3-of-4 other starters back. The Bears also get Tristan Clark—easily Baylor's best player before he went down with a knee injury during the 2018-2019 campaign—another year removed from his knee surgery. Butler said, "I think Tristan is going through the process of recovery and is gaining valuable mental aspects of his life that will translate to the game. I think he will come back stronger. It just takes time."

Butler is cognizant this could be his last run in Waco, "I think this is the year where I'm most looked at as an NBA professional. This is the highest on the draft process."

With the understanding this could be his last chance, he's focused on winning a national title.

He ended his video announcing he was going to return with that lofty goal. To do that, he said they, including himself, have to be "more mature than we were last year. The target on our back is humongous and teams will give us the best shot night in and night out. So much hype around our team; (we) have to keep our eyes set on our goals and what we have to do."

But he's confident the team is on track to do that. He said, "I think we're mature as a team. Look through our routines without the coaches. It's a great feeling when we can do that without the coaches (having to get on us). Guys understand the process and where we're at right now."

During the pandemic, Butler thinks he's gotten a lot better. Still just 20, he's one of the youngest rising juniors in the country. He's now dunking much easier. He said, "The quarantine has helped me out a lot. I was training as a professional and worked out my body for about 2.5 months. Day in and day out it helped it out. It's not like I hit puberty, but I feel like I'm finally coming into my body." ∎

Jared Butler went through the NBA Draft evaluation process but ultimately decided to return to Baylor for his junior season with the primary goal of winning a national championship.

Baylor 82, Illinois 69
December 2, 2020 ▪ Indianapolis, Indiana

REAL AND SPECTACULAR

Baylor Flashes Championship Potential Against Illinois

Anyone still questioning Baylor's national championship pedigree must have gone to bed early. That's a shame because nobody needs to operate on any sleep to recognize the Bears are like the Godfather: somehow the sequel is better than the previous installment.

This victory is wild because the Bears didn't play that well in the first half. Baylor managed just .89 points per possession in the first half — a paltry sum that ranked well below their average of 1.15. Their top five opponent banked a three and another long jumper, which usually portends that the lucky bounces that decide heavyweight bouts are going to doom you; their two best returning scorers went 0-of-6 from deep. And they still beat a top five team by 13.

If there was one question about the Bears entering the season, it's their play at center. Freddie Gillespie earned All-Big 12 honors and made the defense work last year. As then acting head coach Jerome Tang noted after the Louisiana game, "Freddie knew 100% of our ball screen coverages." That knowledge and his quickness and length helped Baylor's defense finish fourth in adjusted defensive efficiency, which was a 71-spot jump from the 2018-2019 campaign. With Gillespie gone, Flo Thamba and Jonathan Tchamwa

Tchatchoua had a major test.

Against Illinois they proved their value. Thamba provided great defense and a couple big scores. Tchatchoua put his athleticism and preparation to use. He finished with nine points and nine rebounds, including six on the offensive end. Davion Mitchell mentioned, a few weeks ago, to me that Tchatchoua provided a new wrinkle on one of their favorite sets because of his ability to throw down lobs. After the game, Mitchell told me that Tchatchoua's philsopohy for Mitchell is to, "throw it as high as you can." The apex of Mitchell's toss proves they understand each other.

Then there's Adam Flagler. He led the Bears in scoring (18 points). The Bears are so rich at the guard position that the most conservative sports fan will countenance the siren call of socialism by arguing for a redistribution of Baylor's backcourt to the less well-off members of college basketball. Seriously, who is Baylor's fourth best guard? I don't want to wade into that debate because these men have performed this well without any slights. The world isn't ready for how good they'd be if they had a legitimate gripe.

Flagler's shown the 3-point line is not a mandate but a suggestion. He frequently fires a couple steps behind it. After the Washington game he told me, "We've been working on our range and everything

Baylor guard Adam Flagler dribbles on the perimeter during the statement win over Illinois. Flagler had 18 points off the bench and was the leading scorer for the Bears in the victory.

because it makes us more deadly as a team the farther out we can shoot." Illinois found out Adam Flagler is the sixth man that Five Guys wanted.

The Bears also showed why their defense remains elite. They rank top 10 in adjusted defensive efficiency on KenPom. Ayo Dosunmu was a preseason All-American. The Bears switched well, and as Mitchell told me, they wanted to make it so, "he couldn't go to his right hand." The second best player in the Big Ten went just 6-of-18 and finished -15 for the game. Whether Mitchell, Mark Vital, Jared Butler or anyone else had him, they made his life miserable and shut down the Illini for key stretches.

The biggest worry entering the game involved how Baylor could defend Kofi Cockburn. Illinois' 7-foot center earned preseason All-Big Ten honors. And the Bears hadn't faced a big man like him since losing Gillespie. Cockburn only played 18 minutes as he battled foul trouble all night. Scott Drew told me that a large reason they limited him is because the guards drove so well to force fouls. That speaks to the synergy of the Bears. When the defense struggles, the offense can go on a 9-0 run in two minutes. And if the offense struggles—like it did in the first half—the Bears can go wild on defense.

Nobody wins a title a month into the season. If that happened, Texas A&M would have real titles listed at Kyle Field, instead of the façade that adorns their not so hollowed ground. It's a long season. If the 2015 Kentucky Wildcats couldn't go undefeated, it's hard to imagine anyone doing it.

The Bears are certainly good enough to win it all though. They have a ways to go and some flaws that will leave them worrying the season might end before the Final Four. But those worries matter because Baylor — a team that played a "C" game for most of the first half, but then came back to beat the No. 5 team by 13 points — showed something tonight: they're good enough to win the NCAA Tournament. ∎

Bears forward Jonathan Tchamwa Tchatchoua throws down the dunk in the win over the Illini, two of his nine points in the game.

23
FORWARD

JONATHAN TCHAMWA TCHATCHOUA

Baylor's Breakout Big Man Discusses Life and Basketball

January 8, 2021

Sometimes it doesn't take long to think disaster is inevitable. And one game into the 2018-2019 season, the Baylor Bears' season looked over. The team fell to Texas Southern at home. Two time zones away at UNLV, Jonathan Tchamwa Tchatchoua played three minutes in a double digit loss to Loyola.

The Bears would find that despair in November — something that perhaps more of us should remember when our preferred candidates lose an election — did not mean much. The Bears rallied to win an NCAA Tournament game.

Tchamwa Tchatchoua would flash plenty of potential that season too. After the firing of Marvin Menzies he'd end up at Baylor and be part of a team that makes anyone taking the field in a "Gonzaga, Baylor or the field" debate someone that should take the first step and admit they have a gambling problem.

But before turning to how a francophone from Cameroon became a key piece on one of the nation's two best teams (we'll save the Gonzaga-Baylor debate for Twitter), let's start in Africa.

Tchamwa Tchatchoua grew up in Dioula, Cameroon. And while he earned a wonderful education there — studying 15 subjects and having class from 8 a.m. to 5 p.m. — he says, "I started learning English at a young age in Cameroon...I wasn't really into it."

That wouldn't seem to be a challenge for him. But at 15, Tchamwa Tchatchoua started playing organized basketball. He says, "I went to this camp in Cameroon. I did okay in this camp. Me and four other guys were selected for basketball without borders. I did alright and got a scholarship to one of the first NBA Global Academy programs in Australia."

Heading halfway across the globe at 15 isn't an easy decision; that kind of move isn't easy for a grown person seeking a reprieve from the drudges of life. Tchamwa Tchatchoua loves Cameroon. But he says, "In Africa, it's more about getting a

Jonathan Tchamwa Tchatchoua didn't start playing organized basketball until he was 15 and his rapid improvement is a big part of Baylor's success.

scholarship to go to the U.S. My dad was all-in to get a scholarship in the U.S. I told him it was my dream...going to Australia was different, but it was backed up by the NBA, so I thought it was a good thing for me."

When Tchamwa Tchatchoua arrived in Australia his problems weren't on the court. He says, "When I got there, when I was first going to class, I didn't understand a word in a single class. I had to go home and teach myself for two or three months. I had to go on YouTube and type all these subjects in French to learn this." For those of us that spend time on YouTube watching mid 2000's rap battles or debates over whether SpongeBob SquarePants is actually about nuclear testing (probably), we can take solace that we maintained a platform that let someone doing real work pass his classes.

After playing in Australia, Tchamwa Tchatchoua achieved his goal and earned a scholarship to UNLV. He went for two main reasons. First, he wanted to play for Menzies — a man who coached another Cameroonian star, Pascal Siakam, while at New Mexico State. The second, and "main reason was wanting to play right away. I only had two to three years of organized basketball...I didn't think sitting out my freshman year would be smart for me. I wanted to make mistakes and learn from it."

Unfortunately, the Running Rebels finished the year 17-14 and made a coaching change. With Menzies gone, Tchamwa Tchatchoua elected to transfer.

He started by looking for a program where he could improve. He said, "I looked at players getting better in their redshirt year, and I considered that I wouldn't get a waiver, so it would maximize potential."

Baylor fit that mold. Ekpe Udoh went from averaging six points per game as a sophomore at Michigan to the No. 6 pick in the NBA Draft after one season in Waco. Royce O'Neale improved in nearly advanced statistical category after leaving Denver and has made tens of millions for the Utah Jazz. And Davion Mitchell, MaCio Teague and Manu LeComte became All-Big 12 players at Baylor after sitting out a year.

Tchamwa Tchatchoua had other reasons that Baylor landed him over Nebraska and Grand Canyon. He credits, "The coaching staff and faith. I realized I kind of lost my faith. I was focused on getting that back. Coach Drew had the same energy and is so positive like I am. I felt like being around a coaching staff built for me."

The Bears' fans may not have been thrilled when they first saw Tchamwa Tchatchoua's UNLV numbers. He averaged three points—while shooting 47% from the field—and three rebounds per game for a mediocre Mountain West cadre. But Scott Drew told me at a press conference they wanted him because, "first and foremost his character and work ethic. We knew he'd put in the time, especially with the year off, he'd get better-and make our team better. Every day he practices so hard, he'd make himself better but also the team better."

Time is only valuable if you do something with it. To those that don't the refrain, "Wait until next year" becomes an annoying ballad of nothingness. Tchamwa Tchatchoua did something with his time. Over that redshirt year he got substantially better by turning to people that could help him.

That didn't make the redshirt year easy. He says, "The first month was tough. They were great Big 12 athletes. Freddie (Gillespie) was a great defensive player. He would always beat me every day. Tristan (Clark) was always that guy you couldn't guard." When facing that kind of situation, Tchamwa

Tchatchoua could have sulked and embraced that maybe he wasn't built for the Big 12, or he could have gotten better. He did and says, "Freddie gave me a lot of tips because we lived together. We watched film every night, and he took me to the gym with him."

The hype around Tchamwa Tchatchoua was intense entering the season. Mitchell told me about lob opportunities, and Clark said at a press conference that, "Jon is super athletic and one of the most athletic players I've played with. He's going to surprise a lot of people. He'll lead the team in rebounding and can defend on the perimeter."

If anyone thought Clark was a liar, they found out he displayed an honesty befitting Abraham Lincoln with Tchamwa Tchatchoua's performance against Illinois. The Bears worked two empty side ball screens for him, and the Illini had no chance.

I asked Mitchell about those lobs after the game, and he said, "We talked about it earlier, and he said, 'throw it as high as you can.' He's got the most bounce in the gym. I don't even think where I throw it up. He just goes and gets it."

Tchamwa Tchatchoua says that he thinks his vertical leap is 40 or 41 inches. To put that in perspective, that's a lot. He says, "I feel like I got more bounce this season. Shout out to Charlie Melton (Baylor's strength coach). Weight training and conditioning have been hard during quarantine with a shortened schedule. Charlie did a great job. he did a great job getting us ready and (boosting) our athleticism."

Those lobs are also the product of strong chemistry between Mitchell and Tchamwa Tchatchoua. He says, "We worked on it during the summer and giving him enough confidence. Whatever he can throw and catching it. It has to be thrown. Now he's one of the best passers I've seen."

Jared Butler is also one of the country's best passers, and he's gotten involved in these lob chances too. After the Kansas State game, I asked him about two alley-oops he threw to Jon. He said, "With Jon you just have to throw it up as high as you can. Not too many people can reach 14 feet. It was back-to-back."

The Bears dealt Bruce Weber his worst loss at Kansas State. After the game, Scott Drew said, "The execution and passes are some great passes, and Jon gives you an opportunity to be off target and get it."

Although he's spent most of his life across the Atlantic, Tchamwa Tchatchoua has mastered American diplomacy. When I asked about the difference between Mitchell and Butler's lob passes, he says, "I'm not trying to be diplomatic, but they're both great passers." He did let me know that "Both them are competing for, 'Jon, which is the best.' They're always asking, 'Which is the best one.'"

A good offensive game is about more than dunking. Tchamwa Tchatchoua has broadened his game. Two plays against Kansas State exemplify that he's more than a dunker. He hit Matt Mayer cross-court, which led to a layup. He says, "I developed that during my redshirt year with Jake (a manager) and all the G.A.'s. They told me that I'm a little smaller compared to some bigs, but when I use my faceup, I can see if they're over playing me from the help side and throw that pass right away."

He also put the ball on the floor and scored. I asked him what he's looking for when he decides whether to attack. He says, "It's about a read. How much focus they put on the guards. They're all great players, so they'll put so much attention (on them). If the defender is focused on the guard, I'll try and attack. I'll try and go inside."

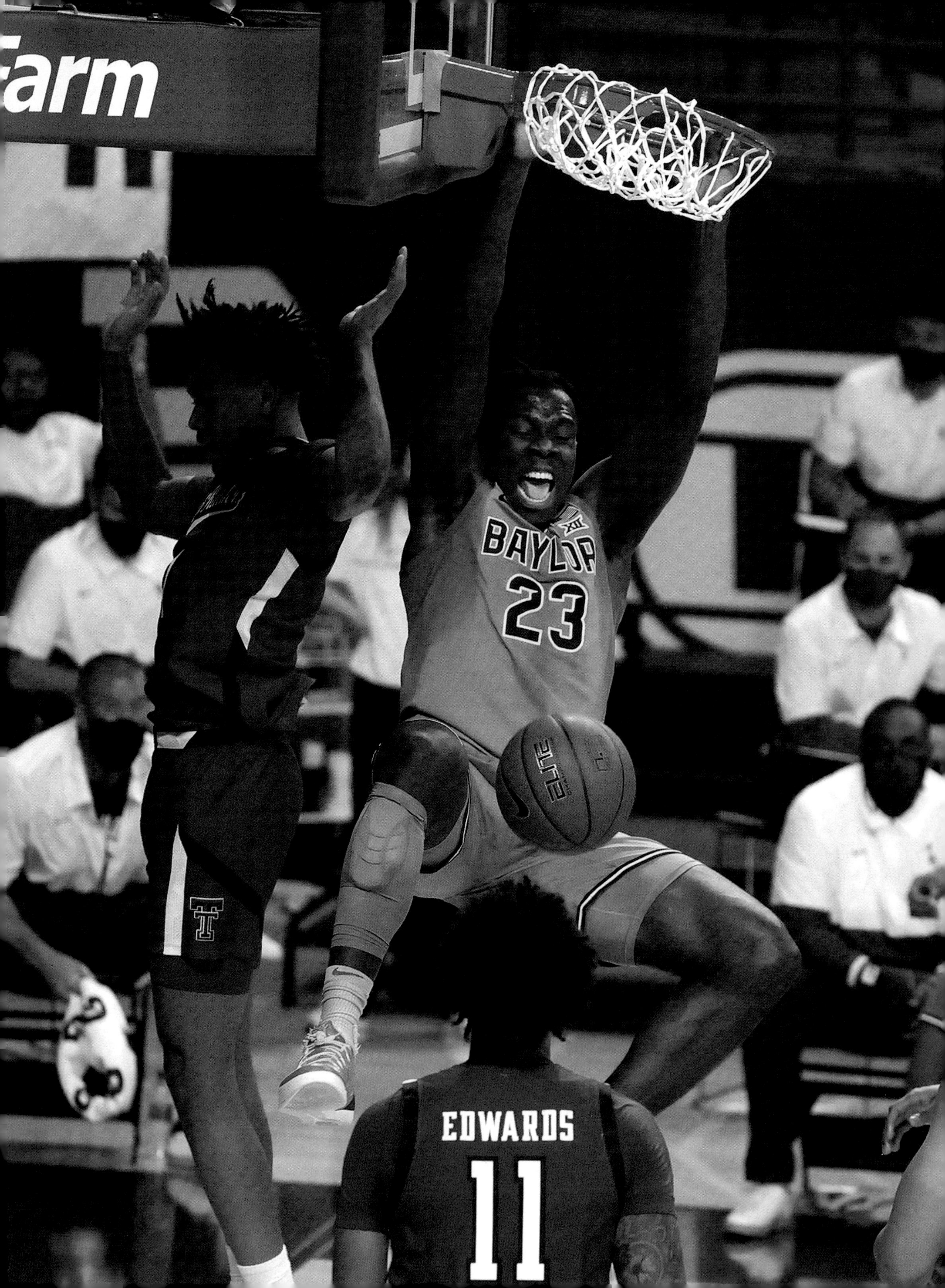
Farm
BAYLOR
23
EDWARDS
11

Although I've never played defense in basketball, Tchamwa Tchatchoua does. The Bears have the No. 5 KenPom defense. If that mark holds, it will be back-to-back top five seasons. With the loss of Gillespie, there were real concerns about whether the Bears could maintain that mark. But Tchamwa Tchatchoua can react quickly and eliminate opportunities:

Against Iowa State, the Bears couldn't make a three. They started 3-of-14, a surprising mark for Baylor's coterie of guards and a team that ranks No. 2 nationally in 3-point percentage.

And with 10 minutes left, the Bears trailed. They had trouble defending middle pick-and-rolls. So the Bears opted to switch screens. After the game, Drew said, "We trust our bigs to guard a guard…it's like a pitcher when you have a fastball, it's great, but it's also good to have the slider, the curve, the knuckler or whatever else. The fact that Flo (Thamba) and Jon can guard a guard helped us out down the stretch."

In one key sequence, Rasir Bolton appeared to have zoomed past Tchamwa Tchatchoua for an easy bucket. But he blocked the shot. He said, "It's about riding hips. I'm good laterally, but I'm still big, and I get beat sometimes. We knew that he loved shooting his layup high, and I knew I had a chance to get there."

Tchamwa Tchatchoua hasn't hit his ceiling either. After their first two games in Vegas, associate head coach (then acting head coach because Drew had COVID-19) Jerome Tang said, "this is a process, it will be mid-January and you'll start to see it come together even better."

In his time at Baylor, Tchamwa Tchatchoua has made lasting friendships. He said that Butler let him know he was returning to Baylor weeks before his announcement.

And he's grown in his faith. He credits the Baylor program, and the JOY motto of prioritization — Jesus, others, yourself — for rekindling his faith. He believes he's on, "the right path."

The setbacks we suffer give us the chance at something better. Some of Baylor's recruiting misses are now at their second schools after they showed they weren't quite ready to play high major basketball, while Tchamwa Tchatchoua is at his second school and thriving at Baylor.

There's nothing quite like the relentless optimism of Tchamwa Tchatchoua. He's half a world away from his home chasing his dream. For now, he says, "I want to win the Big 12 and national championship. I haven't been here three years, but I feel like I've been here 40, and we haven't won a natty. I want to do it."

Maybe that's why Drew said earlier this season, "If every player were like Jon, then everyone would want to be a coach." ∎

Jonathan Tchamwa Tchatchoua finishes strong in a March 7 win over Texas Tech.

24
FORWARD

MATTHEW MAYER

Overcoming Self-Doubt Keyed Forward's Success

January 14, 2021

The narrative about Matthew Mayer — that his overconfidence is why he used to turn down shots as often as an alcoholic on $2 fireball night — is wrong. That's a blunt way to start a profile, but most of the time, we only remember one big narrative about someone or something years later.

In an era of constant information, and an educational system that rewards knowing about something long enough to pass a test, our long-term memories are decimated. And years later, most folks aren't going to remember how well Mayer played defensively against Iowa State — though we'll cover that too — but I hope they remember what he overcame to be this good.

Mayer played high school basketball 14 minutes from Texas, and his mother attended Texas A&M. But he ended up at Baylor. Mayer explains that, "It wasn't that the other schools weren't great. I just thought that Baylor was the best."

During his junior season in high school, Mayer says, "I was ranked No. 1 in the state by all these ranking things. But people don't know this: I always struggled a lot with fear and what people think

about me in the stands, and not feeling like I was deserving to shoot the ball."

That might seem wild to Baylor fans, but Mayer explains, "I got ranked the No. 1 player in the state, and so obviously there's huge expectations that you're supposed to be averaging 35-40 points. I went out and averaged 8.8 points on like 21% from three and nobody thought I was in the top 100, and I didn't think I was in the top 100 anymore. That was super hard for me because in high school all I wanted to do was hide and stand in the corner. (I had a) I didn't want to mess up attitude."

To counter that attitude, Mayer arrived at Baylor and says, "Freshman year it was like, I would force it because I'm not coming back to that. I don't care if I shoot a million shots. I'm not going back to that."

Mayer's mindset put him in a rough spot to open his Baylor career. The Bears lost to Texas Southern, and Mayer says, "I played nine minutes and went 0-for-9 that game [he went 0-for-6, but it's a nice change that in a time of bravado, Mayer remembers a worse performance than happened]. I was upset with myself, and thought, 'man, do I even belong here.' I probably wasn't thinking about the

A top-100 recruit coming out of Austin's Westlake High School, junior Matthew Mayer provides valuable scoring off the bench for the Bears.

team as much as, 'I don't even belong here.'"

Despite his early struggles against Texas Southern, Mayer flashed the skillset that Baylor's staff and so many recruiting services saw. Against Arizona, Mayer ran a middle pick-and-roll and hit Jared Butler for an open three. He says, "Being able to read the opposite side defense, that's part of my game. They'd joke about me shooting a lot — and I do shoot a lot — but I think I'm a pretty underrated passer."

After a rough start for the Bears, the team rallied to win an NCAA Tournament game. He credits their turnaround in the Wichita State game — a contest where they got down 40-9 — and notes, "A lot of guys being mature like Makai (Mason) and Jared came along really quickly — helped carry us to some wins."

Unfortunately Mayer had offseason surgery before his sophomore season. That limited his ability to improve. He says, "I was out for, I don't even know how many months. I was out for like four months. It was a long time. I didn't get to do much. My sophomore summer I didn't really get to do any strength training or conditioning or anything." Although Mayer enjoyed the Bears' trip to Italy, the surgery meant he couldn't play at all on that trip.

His sophomore season didn't start out the way he'd hoped. With Mario Kegler no longer part of the program, Mayer still wasn't playing too many minutes. The thought of transferring crept into his mind early last season. He says, "I wasn't playing with a dude (Kegler) that played 25-30 minutes gone. I was thinking, 'if Rio's gone, what's the point in me even staying. I'm never going to have the chance.'"

Mayer rejected that notion, and elected to stay at Baylor. He says, "if my goal is to be in the NBA, I need to focus on getting to that point. If I'm truly an NBA player, then they'll play me. And if I'm not an NBA player, then I'm just going to spend my career at Baylor."

After showing his potential in a big win against Villanova, Mayer had a fantastic performance against West Virginia. This is probably the most memorable play of Mayer's career.

He says the defender, "was trying to keep me in the corner, so I tried to go straight up, and then I just spun, and the baseline was wide open, and I just happened to dunk it. It wasn't too much of a thought process for me."

That game seemed like a turning point in Mayer's season. He'd played 14 minutes or fewer in the previous 10 games. He says, "I was playing almost none at the beginning of the year...the West Virginia game was kind of a turning point." Over the final six games that he was healthy, Mayer played at least 15 minutes in all of them. He had 19 points on just seven shots in a victory at Kansas State, which earned him KenPom's game MVP.

Mayer actually thinks the West Virginia dunk isn't his best. He says, "My favorite dunk was the one at TCU my freshman year. I was playing really well, and then I got a steal on a fast break. Alex Robinson went under me, and it was so hyped for me. It was the first Big 12 game. That was my favorite."

The Bears were playing well with a variety of lineups last season; there's a reason they were going to earn the program's first No. 1 seed in the NCAA Tournament. One key lineup during that run had Mayer at the four. When I talked to him this summer, MaCio Teague told me, "Four guard lineups can spread the floor a lot. Throw Matt Mayer in there, floor really spreads out and (we have) good opportunities to work."

Mayer would have been healthy for the Big 12 and NCAA Tournament. Unfortunately COVID-19 struck. He says, "We were sitting in the hotel room watching the Mavs game...We're sitting there like

With 17 points in 24 minutes, Matthew Mayer was the Bears' leading scorer in Baylor's win over Wisconsin in the second round of the NCAA tournament.

'the whole NBA got canceled.' And then they called us down for a meeting, so I knew it was canceled. Then we had a season ending talk, and we started chilling the rest of the time. It was pretty tough for us and Freddie and Devonte. That was a tough blow for them."

Coming into the season, Jared Butler told me, "Matt's my roommate. I see him everyday. He's growing as a person...that's going to translate."

I did not realize it, and I don't think Butler meant it that way, but it turns out that was a double entendre. In a great podcast with Ashley Hodge and Jason King of SicEm365, Mayer mentioned that he put on a lot of weight eating Long John Silver's over the summer. I didn't want to press why anyone would eat there when Waco has literally any other fast food establishment, but Mayer says, "I'd be sitting there with my shirt off, and they'd (roommates) be poking my stomach."

He gained the weight, he says because, "There wasn't much thought to it. I was chilling at home, eating everything I could because I was bored. I was chunky." In a description that works in retrospect, but will be the excuse for many when everything returns to normal, he adds, "I didn't look like I was fat. I just looked like I gained somewhat fat, somewhat muscle."

For anyone that's found themselves so big during this catastrophic period that they're using a profile picture from long before we'd heard about social distancing, Mayer provides hope that you too can lose the fat. He says, "I gained a lot of weight during quarantine and Charlie (Melton, the strength coach) helped me out." In the end, he credits Melton for helping him, "turn it into muscle, so it was one of the best things that happened to me basketball wise."

That path from "somewhat fat, somewhat muscle," was, in his words, "like two months of working out back to normal body fat levels. I'm probably lower body fat than I was before."

This season, Mayer's really improved as a cutter. Mayer says, "The weight has helped me because I can cut and (the defender) doesn't bump me as much. I can also jump higher off two feet. Last year I had one or two dunks off one feet. I've had like three this year. It's easier to finish off two, which opens up cutting opportunities for me."

There was also a nice sequence late against Kansas State that shows Mayer's mindset. The game's outcome was assured as a Wildcat went up for a dunk. Mayer came over and offered a hard contest. With not many folks in Bramlage Coliseum I could hear Jerome Tang, Baylor's associate head coach, shout his encouragement and excitement at Mayer for playing that hard until the end. Mayer says, "It's just part of who I am. Everyone wants to compete the whole 40 minutes. I think any player would have done that."

He also proved against the Wildcats that he's improved as a playmaker. In the past, Mayer would look to shoot whenever he could. He says, "they'd be like, 'Matt cut on this this,' but I'd be like, 'No, give me the ball.' I was so stubborn. Don't get me wrong, I'm still going to call for the ball a lot and be ridiculously aggressive, but it's when we have an advantage not do it every time." In that one play against Kansas State, Mayer ended up near the rim but surrounded by multiple defenders. In the past, Mayer might have taken a tough shot. But when LJ Cryer called for the ball, Mayer hit him for a triple.

Mayer's doing a fantastic job balancing his spots this season. He says his biggest improvement this year has been, "Way better decision-making and obviously I'm stronger; all the coaches helped me. It felt like my freshman and sophomore year was being the role player. This year, it's more, 'we want you to be aggressive, but 'we want to show you how to be aggressive.' My freshman and sophomore year I felt like I was fighting, 'do I deserve to be aggressive.' But yeah, I do. This year it feels like, 'we want you to be aggressive. We want you to do these things, but as long as you do, we're okay."

Being a good white basketball player inevitably means baffling comparisons to other white basketball players. That's not actually a problem or social commentary. It's just hysterical how wild and wrong some of these comparisons get. I asked Mayer about these comparisons, and he laughs and says, "I don't understand why people would say Larry Bird. We play nothing alike. I heard Gordon Hayward and Chandler Parsons, those are pretty solid. But Larry Bird doesn't make any sense."

I've long maintained what I tweeted on February 10, 2000: "Matt Mayer is Taurean Prince. They had the same freshman and sophomore years. We can finally end comparing all white basketball dudes to other white basketball dudes!"

So I was pretty excited during the Illinois game when Taurean Prince tweeted out: "#12 on BU is the guy, yes I know.....but #24 is my favorite player"

When I ask Mayer about that, he immediately knew about the tweet. He says, "I thought that was pretty cool, he's a player I see a lot of similarities with myself. He didn't play a lot his first two years. That third year, he was gunning for that sixth man. And I think we both have NBA potential, and he's obviously there. And he's a player I've long looked up to here."

The Oklahoma game might have been the perfect embodiment of what Mayer can do. He finished with 16 points on just eight shots. The most important thing in basketball is making shots, and Mayer sure did that.

He also did well defensively. At the end of the half, Mayer was tasked with defending one side of the floor when Oklahoma ran a pick-and-roll.

When the Bears sent Tchamwa Tchatchoua a bit higher that left LJ Cryer to offer some resistance to the roll man. So Mayer had to make sure a cutter couldn't get a basket, while also leaving himself enough time to recover to a 3-point shooter.

Mayer has really improved his defensive instincts. That makes it easier to defensive rebound, which is why he ranks third among Big 12 players in defensive rebounding rate during league games. He's also notched more steals, timing when he can stunt and leave his man. In one game turning swipe against Iowa State, he picked Solomon Young's pocket, then drove down the court and found Tchamwa Tchatchoua. That led to free throws for Baylor.

That he's achieved all of this from where he was in high school is pretty ridiculous. He says, "When I came to Baylor, I was going to be "Mr. Guy who shoots the ball." People thought I was ridiculously confident. That was overcompensating for a lack of confidence. People don't know that."

But Mayer's glad he went through that journey. From feeling like he wasn't enough, to knowing he's one of the best players on the floor. He's right when he says, "I think it was good for me. I'm glad that I was stubbornly aggressive. That taught me which ways I should be aggressive for the next four years."

And he sums it up well, "Now I'm averaging more points in 15 minutes a game on the No. 2 team in the country (than I was in high school). And it shows me how far I've come mentally...Now I'm a different player. I've changed my mindset since then. I was always a super talented basketball player—anyone could tell you that—it was a mindset change." ∎

Baylor 77, Kansas 69

January 18, 2021 ▪ Waco, Texas

TO BE THE MAN YOU GOTTA BEAT THE MAN

Bears Emerge as Big 12 Favorites with Win Over Jayhawks

Over the last 11 years, Baylor's achieved plenty of milestones. The program's made a pair of Elite Eights and another two Sweet 16s. The Bears have won in Allen Fieldhouse and won 15 Big 12 games. Baylor's been ranked No. 1 three times in the last five years.

But along the way to Baylor becoming the second-best program in the Big 12 over the last 12 years has been the eternal chase against Kansas. Even when the Bears had the best team in program history last year, KU with Udoka Azubuike and Devon Dotson proved too much.

Baylor's had chances, but ultimately, a few close encounters doomed them from usurping Kansas. In 2010, foul trouble ruined them in Lawrence. In 2012, a bad flagrant foul by Baylor let the Jayhawks run away in Waco. And in 2017, the team fell twice in close fashion. Even after a big win in Allen Fieldhouse last year, the Bears couldn't quite finish the job in Waco. Fifteen wins would have won the Big 12 every season from 1997-2019. Unfortunately that tally left the Bears two games behind the 2019-2020 Jayhawks.

Tonight may not be the changing of the guard for more than one night, but I suspect tonight had more significance than a normal January victory. Kansas gave everything it had. The Jayhawks went 10-of-19 from three. A top 15 team should basically never lose shooting that well. While maybe Baylor got sloppy a few times, Kansas played intense defense. That led to 18 Baylor turnovers. The Jayhawks gave everything they had. It didn't matter. The Bears were too good.

The Bears did so many of the things peak Kansas teams used to do. Jared Butler, with another 30-point performance against Kansas, wiped them away. In years past, Kansas could count on Sherron Collins or Frank Mason or Thomas Robinson carrying them in big games. Butler's that player. When I joked with him after the game about why he plays so well against Kansas, he said, "I don't know maybe I don't like blue...I don't know, Kendall." While that answers conveys the levity of trying to explain the unexplainable — how does Butler plays his best when his best is needed — it highlights that he's on a different plane. Kansas used to have the best player in the conference. Baylor does now.

Kansas used to also put teams away with a hard punch back. The Jayhawks cut the lead to single

MaCio Teague scores two of his 13 points in Baylor's win over No. 9 Kansas.

digits on multiple occasions in the first half. Prior Baylor teams — like prior teams throughout the country — might have folded. This one didn't. Down five, the Bears dialed up a different five out look where Mark Vital scored on an alley-oop. I asked Drew about that after the game and he said the ball had been "stagnant," so they wanted to mix things up. When I asked Mark Vital about that play, he credited the coaching staff for finding a way to call the perfect play. Drew went back to that play later in the second half and Jonathan Tchamwa Tchatchoua overpowered Mitch Lightfoot for the bucket.

With the win, Baylor leads Kansas by three games in the Big 12. Texas is only one game back in the loss column. Drew and his staff will make sure the players understand they don't get a trophy for starting 5-0 in conference; last year proved that. But the starters have all been in Waco for at least three years. They understand the perils of blowing a game like they did in Fort Worth last season, and when they fail to play their best — as they did in Ames and Fort Worth — they can still win by double digits.

There's something special about this team. In a normal year, Butler might have accepted the NBA feedback and just been a second round pick. Davion Mitchell — a hounding defender that made life miserable for the Jayhawks' cadre of guards — might have decided he'd spent enough time in college. MaCio Teague, maker of an and-one that ended any hopes for a Kansas miracle, could have gone pro with a degree. And Mark Vital could have listened to some of the advice that told him he needed to start making money. None of them followed that path. Each had individual reasons for coming back, but collectively they knew they could

win the Big 12 title and a national title by returning. That proposition played a role in swaying all of them to return. That culture can lift a program to the spot its chased after a pre-Drew run that would make a class on Baylor basketball's on court history from 1951-2003 last ten minutes.

Drew also coached a fantastic game. Earlier in the season, associate head coach Jerome Tang took the reins as acting head coach. Drew had COVID-19, and Tang led the Bears to a 2-0 record. He said that this was the best staff they'd had in the 18 years of the Drew era. Tonight showed that. When Butler had two fouls, Drew didn't take him out. I asked him about that after the game, and he said, "I don't like to foul out players." The constant innovation led them to take a three point per game scorer from UNLV that provided necessary rim protection. It helped them go all-in to secure Mark Vital when he was a ninth grader so he could make the kinds of defensive plays he had made tonight to stymie Kansas' runs. And it led them to change their offensive play calls by becoming an overwhelmingly middle pick-and-roll team early, and then a different weaving team late.

Maybe this was just one spectacular night for Baylor basketball. But the Bears have the league's best incoming recruiting class, and they have the best team in 2020-2021. At 25% capacity, the Ferrell Center was louder than it was during the 2012 battle that felt like a possible changing of the guard. That one wasn't. This one felt like it was. ■

Mark Vital scores on an alley-oop in the first half.

Baylor 81, Oklahoma State 66
January 23, 2021 · Stillwater, Oklahoma

THE FIVAL

America's Best Lineup Powers Spectacular Win Over Cowboys

After eating an entire medium pizza for dinner, I couldn't tell if my gut was telling me that Baylor was in trouble down 50-48 near the under 12 timeout of the second half, or if my body was ready to shut down for punishing it like that. Baylor had an easy solution for their struggle: throw Mark Vital at the five. That lineup powered Baylor past Oklahoma State 81-66. My body searches for a solution to its travails.

With Cade Cunningham out — he did go through pregame warmups for a minute — this seemed like it might be an easy victory for the Bears. But Oklahoma State had quite the first half. They pushed ahead of Baylor 34-25, which gave Baylor their largest deficit of the season.

In the second half, Baylor couldn't quite pull into the lead. They opened the half with zone fist crack, a play that Kansas used to pound Duke's 2-3 zone in the 2018 Elite Eight. I asked Scott Drew about that play after the game, and he said, "We've run that for several years; we used to play that zone, and they'd (Kansas) run it all the time. The smart take from the strong, and we've run that for years; sometimes it's just more open."

Down 50-48 with 12:22 left, Baylor inserted Mark Vital at the five surrounded by the three starting guards (Jared Butler, Davion Mitchell and MaCio Teague) and Adam Flagler. I dubbed those lineups the Fival — Vital at the five — two years ago when Vital started playing center after Tristan Clark's season ending injury. I also added that name because Fievel is the main character in *An American Tail*, a great movie. The Bears (with a quick interlude of Jonathan Tchamwa Tchatchoua to give Vital a breather) went on a 33-16 run to end the game with that lineup.

That lineup stymies defenses. I asked Davion Mitchell about that cadre after the game, and he said the Fival works, "Because we can switch 1-5; Mark can guard 1-5." Few men can truly defend all five positions; Vital can. With their switching, the Bears don't have to worry about missing a rotation or tagging a rolling big man while a 3-point shooter gets open.

In a classic *Simpsons* episode, Homer runs for sanitation commissioner. He uses the slogan, "Can't someone else do it" for taking out the garbage. The problem for the citizens of Springfield was that someone else couldn't grab your garbage from the kitchen and take it out. Springfield's budget collapsed as the price came due. For most switch everything teams that same problem arises. Eventually teams can feast on one problematic matchup. Usually it's the five man guarding a point guard. And, like Homer's quandary, someone else in the lineup actually can't do it. But in Baylor's

Jared Butler goes to the basket against Oklahoma State. Butler led Baylor with 22 points in the win.

case, someone else can actually do it. The Bears are happy to pass along the defensive assignment to someone else knowing that each member of the five-man lineup can handle the task of defending their newest player.

That lineup eviscerated Oklahoma State. As Scott Drew said after the game, "Normally when you downsize with our 3-point shooting and ball movement, you usually get more on the offensive end. Defensively you have to be able to rebound, and in the second half we were able to do that." Vital tipped key rebounds to teammates. The guards corralled them too, often fueling runs in transition. And if the Bears are in transition, things are going pretty, pretty, pretty good for the Bears.

The Fival succeeds offensively, in large part, because the Bears can run pick-and-rolls with Vital as the screener. When he rolls to the hoop, the Bears get open plays as teams are forced to tag or help off corner shooters to stop Vital from waltzing into the lane for a dunk. I asked Mitchell about that, and he said trying to defend that Fival sequence, "It's definitely hard because we've got all shooters on the court…when he rolls hard he sucks in everybody… one time Jared got the open three from me because Mark rolled so hard everybody collapsed."

Butler also tends to go nuclear in the Fival. He finished with 22 points and was 6-of-7 from beyond the arc. He's shifted the Overton window for national player of the year. Before the debate began and ended with Luka Garza. Now the debate presents the same duality of Gonzaga or Baylor: Butler or Garza for best in the country.

Butler drilled three straight threes, and the students behind me became dejected. I asked Butler if he planned to take the third one regardless, and he said, "Yeah, I guess Kendall. I hit one three, and I was like, 'okay, I'm hot, I should shoot the next one regardless.' That's kind of my mindset overall."

The Bears are not just the Fival. Little plays along the way kept the Bears deficit manageable in the second half. Maybe Baylor still wins if they're down 17 in the second half, but it's better to never have to answer that counterfactual. Tchamwa Tchatchoua sets such quick screens that he can flip them immediately. That ruins the opponents defensive plan because now the screen is going a different way than the planned defense. One of Tchamwa Tchatchoua's flips gave Butler an open 3-pointer in the first half that he swished. Buter told me with Tchamwa Tchatchoua as a screener, "It's kind of like playing hide and go seek. You know how people are on opposite sides of the wall or table? I knew if people go under, I gotta shoot it."

The Fival worked to perfection today. It's reminiscent of when the Warriors would play their death lineups without a true center. Instead, they'd play Draymond Green at the five. The premise was that if the Warriors were just close before turning to those death lineups, everything was over once they went to those. The Warriors' death lineup was nearly unstoppable offensively with so many good dribblers and passers. And they'd be a disaster to score against because of their ability to switch all ball screens. The Fival fits that pattern.

On a day where they were anything but their best rebounding in the first half (Oklahoma State outrebounded Baylor 23-12 in the first 20 minutes), the Bears flipped the switch with their death lineup. Vital played spectacularly, finishing with 19 points on 8-of-9 shooting. And the Bears outrebounded the 'Boys 22-14 in the second half.

As we continue to have the "Gonzaga or Baylor" debate, the Fival remains the ultimate question for the Bulldogs. And with the way Baylor played running it today, it's the question anyone that wants to stop the Bears from winning a national championship will have to answer too. ■

Mark Vital scored 19 points in 27 minutes against Oklahoma State.

Baylor 83, Texas 69
February 2, 2021 ▪ Austin, Texas

BEST BIG 12 TEAM EVER?

After Beating Texas, Baylor Makes Case for Greatest Team in Conference History

No. 6 ranked Texas started 10-of-19 from three and went over 19 minutes without getting called for a foul. Jared Butler, a guaranteed unanimous All-American if the season ended today, drew his third foul in the first half. If ever there were a game to knock off Baylor it was tonight. And despite those problems, Baylor blasted Texas in Austin, 83-69.

The Bears now lead the Big 12 by three games. The two main competitors for the conference are the team Baylor just beat by 14 at their place, or the team (Oklahoma) Baylor beat by 15 when the Bears' two best players went 0-for-8 from three.

This is a hot take to some, but I firmly believe it: The 2020-2021 Bears might be the best Big 12 team ever. The claim seems hyperbolic, but with the weird state of the world during COVID-19, people haven't grasped just how good the 2020-2021 Bears are.

Baylor now sits No. 1 nationally on KenPom. The Bears are +35.54 on KenPom. KenPom began with the 2001-2002 season. In that time, no Big 12 team ranks higher. Not even the 2008 Jayhawks that won the national title and got the boost from winning six NCAA Tournament games. The 2002 and 2003 KU Final Four teams are much lower ranked by that metric. Last season's KU team is too.

The case for Baylor is relatively easy. Baylor went 15-3 in the Big 12 last season and returned four starters from that team. Butler and Mitchell rank as the Big 12's two best players on KenPom, and honestly, I don't think anyone else is close to them. Mark Vital is probably the country's best defender, as he contains guards and then eviscerates opponents down low. They added Adam Flagler this season, a man who scored 49 combined points two years ago as a freshman against UCLA and Marquette. He's the fourth guard on the team and shooting 45% from deep. MaCio Teague played the entire second half against Texas Tech to will Baylor to an eight-point win in Lubbock, and is possibly the best 2-point shooting guard in years. They also have a future NBA player in Matthew Mayer; Mayer is the seventh man right now, and he's shooting 46% from deep. In the 3-point era, Baylor is No. 1 nationally in 3-point percentage and the Bears are a full four percentage points higher than the next ranked high major team (Illinois).

You can make a fine case that the '97 Jayhawks are the Big 12's best team, or that the 2008 Jayhawks deserve that honor because they won the national title. But there's a bias called "Rosy Retrospection" where people tend to recall the past more fondly than the present. It's why the Silent Generation folks remember the 1950s fondly, while they ignore the racism, the Communist threat from the Soviet Union and all the bevy of problems that existed 70 years ago. I think a lot of Big 12 folks that immediately

MaCio Teague scored 10 points in Baylor's win over No. 6 Texas.

deflect the Bears from this conversation are guilty of the same fault: their glorification of the past is blinding them to the reality of the 2020-2021 Bears.

Some would also argue that this is stupid because there are still nine Big 12 games left. The Bears haven't won the league yet. But to me, there's something better about Baylor's position. Gonzaga lurks as a fitting foe. The Bulldogs and Bears are the best teams since 2015 Kentucky. Each gets to measure themselves against the other.

There's also something unique about competing against history. Baylor shouldn't take a game off because this team has a legitimate chance to go down as one of the best teams of the 21st Century. The pressure of history should keep Baylor excited every game and make them more focused on their task. A great but not historic team could justify sleepwalking against Iowa State near the end of the campaign. But this team is playing for something more than most.

Even those that want to argue, "Well, these other teams have pros" are missing something too. Mitchell and Butler are both first round picks in ESPN's latest mock draft. None of the 2008 Jayhawks became NBA All-Stars. Few programs get players as good as Mitchell, Butler, Teague and Vital to all return for their third to fifth years after high school. If Kevin Durant were 22 in college, I'd take the 2010 Texas Longhorns, but we deal with how good are guys when they're still in school. And Baylor's guys are substantially better than the rest of the league.

The Bears could end up losing the Big 12 or get bounced early in the tournament and might make me look stupid. But when you believe something, you should have the guts to say it. I've traveled to Ames, Manhattan, Stillwater, Fort Worth and Waco to watch this team because I realized pretty early on that I'd never cover a team as good as this one again. It's time for the rest of the world to recognize there's a good chance the Big 12's never seen a better one either. ∎

Davion Mitchell led the Bears with 27 points against the Longhorns.

45
GUARD

DAVION MITCHELL

Baylor's Defensive Stopper Develops Offensive Game

February 15, 2021

Davion Mitchell — a man who is from Georgia, who left a college in Alabama, to end up a potential All-American on a team in the heart of Texas — pulls out an iPad to log into Zoom and discuss his season and development with me while I sit at a desk in Kansas City.

Mitchell sports a Band-Aid across his cheek. He tells me, "Yesterday I was playing with my dog, and I got bit by my dog. I was playing with him, and I guess he got too happy and bit me in my face. I got a little cut in my face."

Perhaps Mitchell's dog has provided a clue into how to defend him. Already one of the country's best defenders — and perhaps "one of" is an unnecessary modifier — entering the season, Mitchell's offensive development might be shocking after his first two collegiate seasons. But this season, nobody can stop Mitchell. Well, at least nobody precluded from biting him.

During Big 12 play, he leads the conference in effective field goal percentage and true shooting percentage. In 13 fewer games, he's made more threes than he did all of last season. And he's shooting 49% from beyond the arc, which is over 15 percent higher than last year.

To those that have worked closely with Mitchell, this was inevitable. Matt Gray, one of Baylor's graduate assistants, told me, "We went to a Dallas Mavericks game last year...by the time we got back to Waco, it was like 1:30 or 2:00 in the morning. Davion wanted to get back into the gym and get shots up. He's one of those guys where we have to tell him to go stretch and get in the ice tub. He's going to keep getting them (shots) up."

Every person I've talked to around the Baylor program raves about Mitchell's work ethic. Obim Okeke, a graduate assistant and former teammate of Mitchell's, mentioned to me, "He doesn't do anything crazy. All he does is play video games or to go the gym. That's all he does. What more could you want from a guy? He never parties."

After a solid sophomore campaign, Mitchell had a choice about the NBA Draft. He could go through the process and get feedback and see if a team might buy that he'd shoot better in the NBA

Davion Mitchell blocks the shot of Villanova's Justin Moore during Baylor's Sweet 16 win. Mitchell had one blocked shot and two steals against the Wildcats.

than he had as a sophomore. But Michell says, "First, I just wanted to be able to finish the season out, and I felt like I wasn't ready. I could have shown more. I had more to prove. I'm as good of an offensive player as a defensive player. I wanted to showcase the next year...I got some feedback on things to work on, and got some (work) in the quarantine and it paid off."

During quarantine, Mitchell went crazy working. Jake McGee, a graduate assistant, let me know, "Over the summer when we were really having to scramble for gym time and find one anywhere we could, it was me, Rem (Bakamus, a graduate assistant), Davion, Jon (Tchamwa Tchatchoua), Jordan Turner and Adam Flagler were the people in Waco. We were having to scrounge the city for a gym the city could let us in and also be safe and not be in danger of contracting the virus. Rem would rebound and help Davion however he needed to be helped for a workout."

After those workouts, McGee says, "Davion and Jon would play the most relentless one on one games I'd see in person. Davion would be on all-time offense and make Jon switch at him and go at Jon's head for 15-20 minutes...They'd go to the mid-post and Davion would have to defend 6-9, 240 (pound) Jon in the mid-post; they did that all of June and July for every workout. I just think that, number one, I can't imagine, having played myself, I never had a teammate who would do that and force me to get better like that. It's just awesome to watch them force themselves to get better every day."

Bakamus is a third-year graduate student at Baylor and played some at Gonzaga (he told me that, "played some is generous"). Bakamus says, "His redshirt year, it was obviously big in his development to shoot the ball off the bounce and off the catch at a high level and thousands and thousands of reps and small tweaks (mattered)." He credits Mitchell for "putting in the work studying film."

While working with the staff, Mitchell made a few changes to his 3-point shot. I brought up that last year the ball seemed to sometimes get too close to his head, and he says, "When I'm working out, I notice sometimes the ball hits my head, and that's when I miss. Every time I don't hit the ball with my head, I feel more comfortable. I don't notice it in the game, but I notice it when I'm working out..."

He also focused on a reproducible form where his hand and ball rotation stay consistent. He says he watched a lot of film of Steph Curry this summer. While Mitchell uses a different form, he focused on Curry and "how he was holding the ball and what fingers he was holding when he shot it. I like how he holds the ball. I was holding the ball wrong. My fingertips weren't on it. My palm was on it." And that led to a small problem for him. Gray says, "His guide hand used to flare out a bit."

A few weeks ago, Bakamus says, "I had a memory pop up on my camera roll and it happened to be Davion shooting. (He made) the smallest of tweaks that he wanted to see on video; footwork, being on balance and landing on two feet, and his follow-through with good backspin."

It's not surprising that the practice played off for Mitchell. Some of his best moments come from the team's meticulous work. He says, "Those lobs to Jon in the Illinois game were unique. We worked on it in practice everyday, and we run that same exact thing over and over, and (to) see it happen in a game was really crazy because it was so easy because we worked on it in practice so much, and we work on it so much all the time."

After a recent Big 12 game, I asked him about how he calls for the ball. Most people shout someone's name or say "ball". Or in the case of Matt Mayer, clap for the ball. When I asked Mitchell about the sound he makes to call for the ball, he seemed completely perplexed. Mitchell says, "I didn't even notice until you asked the question."

After I asked him this time, Mitchell says, "I definitely know what you're talking about. I watched the film and you can hear me say, "wo," "wo." I didn't notice that until I started listening with the film, and I normally don't listen to the sound... Coach Drew tells us to yell names if wide open; I just try to make a noise so they hear I'm wide open."

That perspective leads to a key point about basketball and life. We like to assume that every time we're breaking something down that the other person is conscience of everything they're doing. But in the moment we make decisions, we're generally not breaking down every thing we do. Sometimes we're immersed in what we're doing and tuning out the noise.

But that means we're doing something spectacular that comes from reacting to new situations. Mitchell had no idea how he called for the ball. He's so into the game that he didn't understand how he calls for the ball; something he's done thousands of times. His call is one that everyone I talked to for this article knew about, but the man himself didn't.

Fortunately, it works. Mitchell's subconscious helps him; his monosyllabic holler is quicker than screaming a name. In a moment, anyone with the ball has their attention drawn by Mitchell's call. Sure, he sounds like a contestant that will not be going to Hollywood on "American Idol." But that sound gets Mitchell expeditious passes and he correctly notes, "Your teammates are reacting like, 'What's that noise' and react and see you're wide open."

A lot of Mitchell's shooting improvement is due to confidence. As Jared Butler told me, "We told him keep shooting." Bakamus says that last year, "I know his numbers didn't say that...we were in there a good amount of times and we were seeing him make 75, 80 threes out of 100." Despite that success in practice during his redshirt year and last season, Okeke says, "last year if he didn't make a shot, he wouldn't shoot."

That's changed this season. Mitchell says, "It was just a confidence thing. I had to get more confident in my shot. I am shooting more, and I feel like it's going in because I'm confident." In his final 13 games last season, he never attempted more than five threes; strong evidence for Okeke's view that Mitchell would stop shooting when he missed. Eleven times he shot fewer than five triples last season. But over the Bears' last six games this year, he's shot at least five triples on five occasions, including 22 attempts in Baylor's last three contests.

Even with a rough start from three to begin conference play, Mitchell kept shooting. During the first three Big 12 games, he went 0-for-12 from deep. But this year is different. He says, "I wasn't really too worried about it. Everyone's going to have those slump days and slump games. I had to keep working on it and stay confident tin myself. It wasn't really a big deal to me. I'm just going to keep shooting and doing the same things I was doing."

After that 0-12 start in Big 12 play, Mitchell has hit at least 50% of his threes in 5-of-6 games.

He's also become a much better passer this year. Against tier "A" opponents on KenPom — which are the best games — he's assisting on 25% of possessions this season, compared to 18% last year.

With the Bears down at halftime against Oklahoma State, Mitchell did a nice job breaking down Oklahoma State's zone and finding Butler — who was hot from three. Mitchell says bounce passing was, "one of the things we worked on the practices before. We knew they were going to go zone and were really long. We worked on 'bounce passes are going to be wide open.' Especially as you get into the zone because their hands are going to be so high." Between bounce passes and a variety of other dimes, Mitchell finished with nine assists. The Bears left Stillwater with an easy victory.

Figuring out causality is difficult. When you examine two numbers and see both going up, is one acting on the other, or are they totally independent? Mitchell's shooting better from three but also at the rim. Maybe he has more space to work near the rim because defenders respect his shot. Maybe he's shooting better because opponents are afraid when he reaches the rim and playing off of him some. Or maybe he's just improved as a multi-level scorer. Figuring out why Mitchell's so much better scoring near the hoop is a fun debate. But there's no argument that he's a lot better finishing this season. Per hoop-math, Mitchell is making 72.5% of his shots near the basket. That's over 12% higher than last year. It's also easily the best mark ever for a Baylor guard.

Mitchell is quick to credit his big men for that jump. He says, "Last year we weren't really sealing as much. Flo and Jon do a great job; it's an easy lane for me. Instead of two people coming to contest, it's usually no one or one person...we get wide open layups and bigs play a big part of these percentages."

I'd also credit Michell's ability to go left. As a right-handed guard, most guys would prefer to drive with their dominant hand. The Bears used to open games with a clear-out play where Mitchell would drive left. As teams scouted that, the Bears stopped opening every game with that set. But they still look for chances to get Mitchell going left. He says, "I just always enjoy going left. Me being able to go both ways makes it hard to send me one way...usually

right-handed people, they send them left. I love it because I finish with my left as well as my right, and I think it's a good thing to be able to go both ways."

In the last two Big 12 games before a COVID-19 pause, Mitchell's exploded. He finished with 29 points on 7-of-9 shooting from three against Kansas State. That helped Mitchell earn Big 12 Player of the Week honors. He's also made the Naismith Watchlist for the top 30 players in the country.

If anyone expected a drop-off, the Texas game proved that expectations aren't reality. Displaying those skills that make him a good rim scorer, Mitchell made a reverse layup against Andrew Jones. I thought maybe it was just easier for Mitchell to lay it up without reversing, but I have a vertical leap that proves the movie "White Men Can't Jump" has an accurate title. So Mitchell told me, "I think the angle I was at, I had to go reverse; he probably would have blocked it, or it would have been a harder shot to take; it was like the perfect angle for a reverse layup, and I knew I already had the step on him. And he was either going to foul me, or I was going to make that layup like I did."

In the second half, Mitchell stopped immediately to hit a 2-point jumper. Not long after, he found himself in the air with the Longhorns turning their heads to focus on him like a performer on 6th Street can only hope their act elicits. Mitchell says, "If I shot it, it was going to be a really good contest. I should have stayed on my feet. I was looking to pull. When I went to the middle of the lane, people are looking at me...I hit Adam (Flagler) a lot on those slide threes, so he knew it was coming; he was all ready for the shot and is always shot ready."

After this incredible start, Mitchell is earning plenty of accolades. He appears on just about every 2021 NBA Draft board, including as a first round pick on ESPN's mock. If the season ended today,

Davion Mitchell was named the Naismith Defensive Player of the Year as the country's best defender for the 2020-2021 season.

he'd easily earn First Team All-Big 12 honors. The only thing that will stop him from making a first or second team All-American list is if an outlet foregoes naming two Baylor players.

He should keep getting better too. He wants to get to the free throw line more and reduce his turnovers. Improving in those areas shouldn't be a problem, given his work ethic and natural ability. He came to Baylor a phenomenal defender — earning the moniker "off night" from Baylor associate head coach Jerome Tang because all the guys he guards seem to have an off night. But he'll leave as one of the top five players in the last 20

years of Baylor basketball because of how he's improved offensively.

It will be fun to see just how much Mitchell can keep improving, and where that takes him this season and eventually in the NBA.

One more story explains why I'm not betting against him reaching incredible heights. Bakamus told me, "I got him a Kobe Bryant book last year; it kind of backfired on me because now he wants to send me quotes about Kobe at random times of the day. And he'll open up a page and want to get in the gym instantly, and he doesn't want to take days off because Kobe didn't take days off." ∎

Kansas 71, Baylor 58
February 27, 2021 ▪ Lawrence, Kansas

AWFUL NIGHT ENDS PERFECTION

In Second Game Back from Three-Week COVID-19 Pause, Bears Fall to Jayhawks

In its second game back from COVID-19, Baylor played its worst game since losing to Washington in November of 2019.

The Bears were not good. Scott Drew said after the game, "We had three weeks where we got worse. They had three weeks where they got better. We gotta catch up."

The Bears entered the game No. 1 nationally in 3-point shooting. They went 6-of-26 from deep. Baylor has the nation's best backcourt. The four guards shot 28% from the field on a terrible 15-of-52 shooting.

Jared Butler had been amazing in the first meeting, dropping 30 points on 7of-9 shooting from deep. He scored 31 his freshman season here, and added 22 in the program's first ever victory in Lawrence last campaign. But he scored zero points in the first half and had just five points on 1-of-7 shooting from deep.

The defense fared the worst. Baylor ended up outrebounded 50-28. Kansas scored 1.2 points per possession against a defense that ranked No. 1 in the country in late January. Now the defense ranks No. 17. The Bears couldn't stop the Jayhawks inside, as David McCormack went off for 20 points on 10 attempts.

If Kansas hit some threes, this could have gotten far uglier than the 71-58 final. The Jayhawks went 3-of-16 from deep, and plenty of those looks were wide open. Ochai Agbaji and Christian Braun went a combined 1-of-10 from deep. That's well below their normal rate, and their 9-of-13 shooting from beyond the arc in Waco.

Despite all of the above being true, the Bears still have plenty of reasons to leave fans optimistic. They just went through a 21-day pause. Jonathan Tchamwa Tchatchoua was in his first game back from the COVID pause, and his energy wasn't there. Foul trouble hampered the Bears. It didn't doom them, but Mark Vital and Butler were off the floor far more than Baylor wanted. The Jayhawks shot 10 more free throws. That's not a claim that the refs doomed Baylor. They would have lost regardless of whether a few calls flipped. But most nights Vital, Butler and Matthew Mayer won't be in a tough foul situation, and the Bears won't have their opponent in the bonus so early.

Baylor also had a chance to win this game.

Davion Mitchell reacts after being called for a foul during the second half of Baylor's loss to Kansas.
(Amy Kontras/USA TODAY Sports)

Down 57-52, the Bears got three straight stops. They missed wide open triples. The Bears have been good when they make their run and put pressure on the opponent, but they could never quite rattle Kansas.

All of the Bears' goals remain in front of them. MaCio Teague, obviously upset about losing, mentioned after the game that the team's goal was not to go undefeated. The goal is to win the Big 12 and a national title.

The Bears provided a much better window into how good they are with their performance before the pause. Maybe it will take longer to get back to normal. Baylor's defense is incredibly dependent on making the correct switch and understanding when help is necessary. The Bears botched plenty of those situations tonight. With time to redevelop chemistry, they shouldn't going forward.

Even after such a crushing loss, Baylor still wins its first ever Big 12 title with a win in any of their next three contests. Tonight's performance would leave Baylor an underdog in all three, but tonight's performance is a clear outlier that can largely be attributed to COVID, and Kansas playing quite well.

Nothing is over or doomed. The Bears still have the Big 12's best player and two of the league's top three defenders. Teague's 3-point shot appears back, as he drilled a triple, then provided a 4-point play the next time down the floor.

Kansas is also a good team. I said before the season that Kansas would finish fourth in the Big 12, but make the Final Four. McCormack is playing like the guy Bill Self said would be their best player. And they have quality guards and a ferocious defender in Marcus Garrett. This isn't losing to a terrible team.

Plenty of title teams lose by double digits on the road too. North Carolina won the NCAA Tournament as a No. 1 seed in 2017; they fell by double digits to Georgia Tech and Miami — both worse than this Jayhawks squad. Villanova lost by 23 to Oklahoma in 2016, and then beat the Sooners by 44 in the Final Four. One game doesn't guarantee anything in college basketball, but with the single elimination format of the NCAA Tournament, tonight is a powerful reminder for how painful the ending is for so many teams.

Tonight wasn't good enough. This the best team Baylor's ever had, and the Bears understand so many of them came back to try and win titles. That's still possible. They can use tonight to fuel them for that possibility and leave this a footnote on what can still be the best ending in school history. ■

MaCio Teague led Baylor with 18 points against the Jayhawks. (Amy Kontras/USA TODAY Sports)

Baylor 94, West Virginia 89
March 2, 2021 ▪ Morgantown, West Virginia

FIVAL GOES EAST
How Baylor Basketball Won the Program's First Big 12 Title

As time ran out, Scott Drew hopped on Mark Vital's back to celebrate Baylor's 94-89 win over West Virginia to clinch Baylor's first conference title since 1950 — so long ago that the Korean War had not begun. Baylor is the first non-Kansas team to win an outright Big 12 title since 2004.

Coming off a 21-day COVID pause, Baylor hadn't looked like Baylor in its two return games. They trailed Iowa State, a winless Big 12 team, by 15 points. Kansas, a squad Baylor blitzed by eight points in January, beat Baylor by 13 on Saturday.

With eight players contracting COVID in February, the question remained: would Baylor ever get back to what it was? That question became pressing as the best team in school history needed one win in its final three games to clinch the league.

Down 50-43 with 12 minutes left, and then 60-55 with 8:42 remaining, Baylor had a gigantic challenge. No. 6 West Virginia had won six of seven games; their lone loss was in double overtime to Oklahoma. Sean McNeil finished with 18 points and started the second half 3-of-4 from deep. Over the first eight minutes of the second half, West Virginia scored 2.1 points per possession; Baylor would have been better off surrendering the guaranteed two points of a dunk than what the Mountaineers averaged by torching from beyond the arc.

Facing such a monumental task, Baylor went to a lineup that carried them so many times. The Fival, with Mark Vital at the five, lifted Baylor in those key stretches. With increased spacing, the Bears hit needed triples. Davion Mitchell swished one to make it 60-58.

Unable to get many stops, Matthew Mayer ran near the sideline and flipped the ball over his shoulder to Davion Mitchell, which led to a layup. I asked Mayer about that after the game, and he said, "I just tipped it and didn't even know if one of my teammates would be there." That's how this team operates. A belief that someone else on the team will be ready to meet the moment someone else provides.

That leads to Baylor's defense. The Fival works because, as Davion Mitchell told me last month, "We can switch all ball screens." That means players have to beat Baylor's defenders one-on-one. Baylor didn't get many stops today. Between the pause and West Virginia shooting so well that Virginia will approach West Virginia to consider reunification, the Bears looked too decimated to contain the Mountaineers. But late in the game, the Bears were

Davion Mitchell scored four points in the final minute of overtime to seal Baylor's win over West Virginia in Morgantown.

able to switch on the perimeter and prevent McNeil and others from getting shots.

In one key sequence, Mark Vital stripped the ball leading to a bucket. After the game, Scott Drew found Vital to celebrate. Drew joked about the fifth year senior, "Well, Mark's the only one who's been here longer than me."

Jared Butler finished with 25 points. With 2.2 seconds left, he drove into Derek Culver and made a layup to force overtime. He said, "We ran a slip ball screen. I saw the lane, and I was just like, 'is he trying to take a charge, is he in the charge circle?' I just thought, 'I'm going to jump as high as I can and finish the charge process, and that's my thought process.'"

But with 1:15 left in overtime, Butler picked up his fifth foul. After that, he said, "I just couldn't watch the game. I was praying with coach Charlie (Melton) in the tunnel."

With Butler gone, Davion Mitchell took over. He made a layup, and then notched two free throws. With the additional space, Mitchell proved too quick to stop in the paint.

Down the stretch, everyone came up big. MaCio Teague added a clutch layup to keep the game within a score. Vital offensive rebounded and had a put-back in overtime. After he told Ashley Hodge and Jason King of SicEm365 earlier in the week that Baylor wasn't tough enough against Kansas, his Bears were tonight. Once in the first half, they corralled four offensive boards on one possession.

Even outside of the Fival, the other Bears came to play. Flo Thamba's adept seals — which gave open driving lanes for Baylor's guards — helped Baylor race out to a 21-9 lead.

When the game goes to overtime, every basket matters. That also makes Jonathan Tchamwa Tchatchoua's dunks early in the first half integral.

Plus there were Adam Flagler's two free throws to clinch the game.

That Baylor felt comfortable going small late is a testament to Scott Drew and his staff. West Virginia had Derek Culver, perhaps the only non-Baylor player with a case for Big 12 Player of the Year. The 6'10 junior scored in double figures in his nine previous games. Despite the additional five minutes from overtime to accumulate more points — and after allowing 6'10 David McCormack to score 20 points on Saturday — Baylor held Culver to nine points.

The Bears understand they're not all the way back. After the victory, Butler was asked about the COVID pause and said, "I didn't really think it would hurt us." But they all recognized they haven't quite been themselves, because he said, "That pause really killed us...you lose some in-game shape." Scott Drew added "The pause we had was the toughest one you can come back from."

Baylor came back from the pause and won the Big 12 in the No. 6 team's arena. Several of Baylor's men passed up the chance to be millionaires to achieve this feat.

Now that they've won a conference title — something no Baylor team had done in 70 years — they'll focus on getting right for the NCAA Tournament. They'll do so buoyed by this win, and with added confidence to their belief they can do something no Baylor team has ever done: win the NCAA Tournament. ■

Baylor players celebrate on the court after the Bears' overtime win over the Mountaineers. With the win, Baylor clinched the program's first Big 12 title.

Baylor 81, Oklahoma State 70
March 4, 2021 ▪ Waco, Texas

OFFENSE PEAKING AT THE RIGHT TIME

Bears top Cowboys Behind Scoring from Butler, Mayer

No. 3 Baylor beat No. 17 Oklahoma State 81-70 behind another elite performance by the offense. Maybe that shouldn't be surprising, but in a ton of stories about how phenomenal Baylor's been, the offense's dominance has gone under the radar.

Scott Drew builds dominant offenses. Since 2008, the Bears have ranked top 25 in adjusted offensive efficiency in all but two seasons. Duke is the only other team to do that.

Before the season, Jerome Tang, Baylor's associate head coach, served as acting head coach because Scott Drew had COVID-19. He mentioned the offense was way ahead of the defense. He said, "I'm not worried about our offense."

In a war over analytics or eye test, all sides can agree that Baylor has the best offense in school history. By adjusted offensive efficiency, Baylor ranks 4.5 points per 100 possessions better than its next best offense (2010).

The Bears have now scored 1.25 and 1.17 points per possession in their last two games. Those are unbelievable marks, especially for a team coming off the pause.

Baylor ranks No. 1 nationally in 3-point percentage. The Bears drilled 9-of-22 threes tonight. Jared Butler went 4-of-7 from deep; he's basically locked up Big 12 Player of the Year. MaCio Teague

added a pair, including a tough transition three as Cade Cunningham brought the Cowboys within single digits. He also meandered through Oklahoma State's zone, adding a pair of layups that eviscerated the Cowboy's hope of a comeback in the second half.

Innovation is necessary in sports. Teams take away your best sets, and coaching staffs need to find new ways to get their best players the best opportunities to score. In the first half, Jared Butler hit Jonathan Tchamwa Tchatchoua for a lob.

I asked Butler about that after the game, and he said, "Jon's been asking for a lob for a long time. He said, 'I miss getting lobs.....' We got him one tonight."

Scott Drew said, "That's one of our plays, and he did a great job catching it, and it was a great pass."

That play works because Flagler sets a timely back screen. That set is sometimes referred to as "Spain" because the Spanish national team used those kinds of screens to perfection. That fits Baylor's early season pattern of getting Tchamwa Tchatchoua empty, or on one side of the floor where there's nobody else to defend him. That means there's not a guy that can bump into Tchamwa Tchatchoua and stop his roll to the hoop. And with Flagler's back screen, the defense is already scrambling to adjust to even stopping their side of the field.

A lot sticks out tonight, but let's focus on two

MaCio Teague scores two of his 19 points against the Cowboys.

other areas. First, Matthew Mayer has been on a tear in the last two games. He scored 18 points in Morgantown and made every shot he took in the second half at West Virginia. Tonight he added 19 points on 10-of-13 shooting. He can be unstoppable with his 6'9 frame and handle. He pairs that with an elite jump shot (45% from three on the season).

Finally, there's Butler. He has 47 points and 11 assists in his last two games. After forcing overtime with a made layup with 2.2 seconds left on Tuesday, he added two dunks tonight.

I asked Butler about that after the game, and he said, "He (the defender) came over kind of wanting to take a charge. And I just gotta jump as high as I can, and that was it."

Mayer and Butler are roommates, and will both be millionaires by the time they're 23. In the interim, the duo have a competition over who can finish the season with more dunks.

In a classic Seinfeld episode a child in a hospital wants two home runs from Paul O'Neil, then a New York Yankee. Kramer relays that promise to O'Neil, and he balks. He knows that's nearly impossible against the best pitchers in the world. Maybe Drew understood the specter of O'Neil's two home runs and managed expectations better. He said, "I asked him (Butler) for one dunk before the game; he delivered two."

There's a mood for this team that works. They enjoy the levity of the sport. Basketball should be fun. All of the men on scholarship would like to play professionally, and the coaches all desire that for the players. Each of them also face the pressure of knowing how good they are, and the unending desire to win. But despite the anxiety that could induce, Drew, Mayer and Butler can laugh it up and create funny contests or expectations. If you watch my questions above, it's obvious I'm fairly nerdy (fairly might be doing a lot) and enjoy the quantifiable elements of basketball. But Baylor has a chemistry

beyond all that. That's the beauty of the game. When you crunch all the numbers, you're left knowing something remains. In Baylor's case, it's the bond the men share. That bond is forged over the multiple seasons all of Baylor's rotation players have been in Waco. They've suffered the heartbreak of losing a Big 12 title against Kansas last year, and the high of winning a Big 12 record 23 straight games. They've listened as their coaching staff gathered them in a Marriott and informed them the NCAA Tournament was cancelled. And they've won the school's first conference title since before the Korean War.

The Bears have a greater bond that allows them to have the difficult conversations too. Mayer played just five minutes against Kansas. He said post-game tonight, "(I) had a real talk with Coach Drew about playing time. I had five minutes...(he) let me play through more stuff today...when I get to play a couple more minutes, I get in a groove and appreciate it."

Drew gave Mayer that freedom the last two games. Multiple times this season, Drew's acknowledged he's always improving as a coach too. He doesn't believe he's solved basketball because he's completed the greatest building job in the history of college basketball. He strives to get better every day, and with Mayer, he had a real and deep meeting about the best way to help him succeed. That led to two exceptional performances. Both were integral to Baylor's wins. The Bears certainly lose without Mayer's efforts in Tuesday's overtime win in Morgantown, and they might have lost tonight too.

Add this offense, and the chemistry Baylor has, and Baylor should achieve Mayer's goal. He said after the game that among Baylor teams, "We want to leave a legacy as the best team ever."

They've done that already, and with what they've shown since after COVID-19 left eight of them sidelined, they just might end the season as the best team too. ∎

Baylor defenders look to stop Oklahoma State guard Avery Anderson III in the first half.

Baylor 88, Texas Tech 73

March 7, 2021 ▪ **Waco, Texas**

ONE TRUE CHAMPION

Baylor's Core Four Powers Another Victory

As confetti poured over the middle of the court, MaCio Teague — fresh off the greatest shooting day in Baylor basketball history (10-of-12 from deep) — took the microphone on senior day. He finished his speech saying, "We not done yet."

The Bears don't appear close to done. They'll head to Kansas City the clear favorites to win the Big 12 Tournament, as betting sites make them a 4:7 favorite to win the conference tournament. Baylor finished the season with an 88-73 victory over Texas Tech.

Despite playing four fewer games than some Big 12 teams, Baylor won more games than any Big 12 team. The Bears finished undefeated at home for the first time in the Drew era too.

This was quite a turnaround from last Saturday. The Bears fell to Kansas 71-58 in the Bears' second game back from COVID-19. The Bears seemed a step slow. MaCio Teague met with the media after the Kansas loss and said, "Sometimes your shots don't fall."

Today they did. The Bears were 15-of-24 from deep. Teague finished with 35 points, his Baylor career high. He started 10-of-11 from three. With his performance today, Baylor has six players that finished the regular season shooting at least 40% from deep.

On a day of celebration, the Bears honored their seniors. Tristan Clark went through the festivities after medically retiring before the campaign. He said, "I didn't finish my career the way I wanted, but I'm glad I found a second home in Waco. Sic 'Em Bears!"

Vital had a fantastic day too. Donning a facemask after an injury, he finished with 10 points and 15 rebounds — perhaps the ideal Vital statline. He locked up Mac McClung to prevent Tech from making a run in the second half.

Jared Butler and Davion Mitchell also had good days. They haven't made a decision on whether to go pro, but with both slotted as first round picks on NBA mock drafts, there's a good chance this was also their final game in Waco. The pair combined for 35 points and 12 assists.

The core four of Mitchell, Butler, Teague and Vital started 46 regular seasons games at Baylor. They finished with 42 wins, which equals a 91% win percentage. They ended a 71-year history without a conference title at Baylor. They'll earn the school's first No. 1 seed in the modern era too.

Beyond that, they've set the program on a path

Head coach Scott Drew reacts as his team scores during the second half of Baylor's victory over Texas Tech in the regular-season finale at the Ferrell Center.

to sustained success. They helped recruit Adam Flagler, a possible Big 12 Sixth Man of the Year. And they had the kind of success that helped Drew and his staff secure one of the best recruiting classes in the country next year.

They overcame a COVID pause and the loss of a chance to win a national title last season when the season ended abruptly. The season may end with heartache in March. Gonzaga, Baylor, Michigan and Illinois have solidified No. 1 seeds. At least three of them are going to have a devastating end to the campaign.

Regardless of how it ends in March or April, they've completed the best regular season in Baylor basketball history. That core fueled a new culture, and new expectations. Baylor's athletic director Mack Rhoades took the microphone as the celebration started and said, "The best basketball coach in the country, Scott Drew."

Inspired by the season, Drew shouted out each coach and player as they took turns climbing the ladder to remove the nets in the Ferrell Center. With where the four have taken Baylor, Drew said, "We promise you it won't take 71 years next time."

With where Drew's taken the program, that seems like a safe bet. ■

MaCio Teague drives during the second half. On Senior Day, Teague tied a school record with 10 three-pointers and finished with 35 points.

Baylor 74, Kansas State 68
March 11, 2021 ▪ Kansas City, Missouri

CHAMPIONSHIP OFFENSE

Despite Turnovers, Bears Top Wildcats to Advance

No. 2 Baylor (22-1) knocked off a much-improved Kansas State (9-20) 74-68 and advanced to take on Oklahoma State.

The Bears remain as dominant as ever offensively. Baylor entered the game No. 3 in adjusted offensive efficiency. Since the COVID pause, the Bears have been electric on that end and rank in the top five.

Once again, Baylor performed admirably on offense. The Bears had too many turnovers (21), including 13 in the first half. But the Bears scored a solid 1.14 points per possession. Davion Mitchell and MaCio Teague combined for 47 points. Jared Butler didn't have his best day — he struggled to make layups and had an uncharacteristic seven turnovers — and still finished with 18 points. It's a good sign that Baylor turned it over this much, and its best player didn't have his best day, and they still had an efficient outing.

Baylor's goal this season is winning a national championship. That's the standard Baylor's realistically striving for; that's an incredibly high bar. With Gonzaga, Michigan and Illinois as talented as any cadre of No. 1 seeds ever, at least three, and quite possibly four (including Baylor) are going to be disappointed when they lose for that final time in Indianapolis.

To achieve that lofty goal, Baylor's defense has to get better. Before the pause, Baylor ranked No. 9 in Bart-Torvik's adjusted defensive efficiency. The Bears suffocating defense ranked No. 1 in the Big 12. They turned over everyone, which fueled an offense that probably wasn't as good pre-pause as it is post-pause. In the five games since the pause, and before playing Kansas State, Baylor ranked 190th in adjusted defensive efficiency.

Things didn't go much better tonight. Kansas State's Davion Bradford scored 18 points in the first half. Most of those were on easy layups or dunks. That tied a season high for a full game. In the second half, the Wildcats got a variety of open triples. Nigel Pack, the Wildcats' best player, went 5-of-8 from deep. The Bears let him get open too many times.

There are a bevy of defensive issues. Baylor's defense is designed to force guys to drive baseline. The big man should then be there ready to help. Often the big man is late, which leads to easy buckets. When the big man does get there, the guards aren't there to provide a second line of help or to help the helper. And they've missed boxing out certain guys, letting easy offensive rebounds proliferate.

Baylor understands the defense has to be better. After the game, I asked Davion Mitchell about

Davion Mitchell drives to the basket during the first half against Kansas State. Mitchell scored 23 points in the quarterfinal win, bested only by MaCio Teague's 24-point effort.

what has to improve defensively. He picked up a giant charge in the first half, and he rightfully won Big 12 Defensive Player of the Year. He told me, "I feel like we're not talking enough...on the ball I'm pretty good. Off the ball, I've got to stop helping off the corner. Little errors, we need to fix, and we will do it."

Scott Drew also understands that the Bears have to get better on that end. I asked him about the issues today, and he said they were both some of the ones the Bears have had since the pandemic and some unique ones tonight. He added that KSU is a "tough prep team. Coach Weber has a million sets. They execute so well. That's one of those teams that's difficult when you don't have prep time because they can make you look bad with a million sets."

The Bears can be as good on defense as they were pre-pandemic. Mitchell, Mark Vital and Butler all made the Big 12's defensive team. Jonathan Tchamwa Tchatchoua is swift, which helps him draw charges or pressure the ball. Teague's been difficult for anyone to score again. Thamba did a pretty good job in the second half defending the paint.

How well Baylor can play on defense remains the issue for Baylor winning a national title. The Bears might lose an NCAA Tournament game on an off shooting night, given the variance dictated by the sport crowning its champion at the whims of a single elimination format. But the Bears have a sufficient sample size to show they are one of the country's three best offenses. ■

Baylor players gather at midcourt after beating Kansas State to earn a spot in the Big 12 Tournament semifinals.

Oklahoma State 83, Baylor 74
March 12, 2021 ▪ Kansas City, Missouri

POOR SHOOTING DOOMS BAYLOR

Bears Finish 6-of-28 from Behind the Arc in Loss

No. 2 Baylor (22-2) fell to Oklahoma State (20-7) 83-74. While the defense remains an issue, the biggest impediment to Baylor's success tonight was simple: the Bears were awful from three.

The Bears entered the game No. 1 in 3-point shooting. They've been great from beyond the arc all season. Last Sunday MaCio Teague went 10-of-12 from deep. As Baylor's defense has been mediocre to maybe even bad since the return, the Bears have masked those issues by drilling triples.

Tonight Baylor couldn't hit enough threes. The Bears finished 6-of-28 from three. They missed 16 in a row. Despite good looks, the Bears couldn't convert them.

Baylor's inability to hit threes doomed them. The Bears have some real issues right now. The defense struggles to contain straight line scoring. Avery Anderson, Cade Cunningham and Isaac Likekele got to the rim too easily. That trio is as good as any the Bears will face, but the issue is that the Bears have to beat teams better than Oklahoma State to win the title.

Davion Mitchell played a spectacular defensive game. He made Cade Cunningham's life a disaster.

But after taking a 60-52 lead with eight minutes left, Oklahoma State got Cunningham pretty good looks. As MaCio Teague said, "He got free from our best defender." Once that happened, he hit two step-back threes to make it close enough.

Tonight showed the heartache of the NCAA Tournament. As Scott Drew said after, "In a 40-minute game, anyone can win." If the Bears shoot 10-of-28 — still well below their season average — they win this game. They had plenty of good looks. As Teague noted, "(We) just didn't make shots." Baylor was good enough to beat Oklahoma State nine days ago. They weren't tonight.

The Bears can recover from this. Mitchell-Butler-Teague form the best starting trio of guards in America. They hopefully won't have another shooting night like this. If they do after the first round, it's probably the end of the season.

Baylor's work over 24 games, including a Big 12 title, puts them in position to make tonight's heartache irrelevant. They'll head to Indianapolis as a No. 1 seed. The first opponent will be completely outclassed by Baylor. But as Teague said, "We were a one seed in this tournament and just lost."

Vital feels confident Baylor can rebound. He said,

Forward Flo Thamba dunks during the first half against Oklahoma State. Yet it was the Bears' inability to deliver on 3-pointers that sent them packing from the conference tournament.

"I'd much rather my guys feel this loss." He added, "We needed that loss in a way." He felt like the team overreacted to winning the Big 12 and felt invincible. Now they have a taste of one season ending.

After a loss to a top 15 team, Baylor said all the right things. They know what they have to do. The question remains if they can do it. They showed they could before the break. They've been good enough to win most of their games since it. If they can get back to what they were before the break they can still win the title. If not, they're probably going to lose in the Sweet 16 or Elite Eight. Baylor's played a lot like Iowa since the break—a great offense that can carry a mediocre defense until the offense goes from great to good.

With the best roster and coaching staff in program history, Baylor has a chance to get it all fixed. We'll spend plenty of time analyzing how much Baylor can ride their three starting guards or if the bench can return to playing competent offense. We'll wonder if the defense can get back to its previous level too. But ultimately this is a prove it sport. The burden is on the Bears. And despite tonight's loss, they'll probably never have a better chance to win a national title. Time to seize it. ◼

Oklahoma State's Cade Cunningham battles for the ball with Baylor's Mark Vital, Davion Mitchell and Jonathan Tchamwa Tchatchoua.

Baylor 79, Hartford 55
March 19, 2021 ▪ **Indianapolis, Indiana**

A DEFENSIVE RENAISSANCE

Bears Dominate Hartford in Pristine Performance

Baylor hadn't looked like Baylor on the defensive end. Since the return, the Bears ranked 190th in adjusted defensive efficiency. A mark good enough to make Baylor the possibility of Baylor joining Virginia as the only No. 1 seed to lose to a No. 16 seed a possibility.

With that framework in mind, Baylor faced a daunting task when Mark Vital picked up his second foul with 18:19 left in the first half. The Bears trailed 10-8 not longer after, and as the team clanked enough threes to start 1-of-8 from distance, things felt a bit tense.

Tension can be a lie, and it was this afternoon. Baylor finished the first half allowing just .525 points per possession. The nation's worst offense scores .792, which makes that an impressive feat.

In the seven games since returning in late February, Baylor gave up at least one adjusted point per possession. Today, Hartford scored just .711 adjusted points per possession. So for anyone saying, "Come on, it's a No. 16 seed!" they're missing that even the adjusted stats showed a different result.

Baylor was pristine in so many areas. They pressured Hartford, leading to 24 turnovers. MaCio Teague and Scott Drew both credited getting to practice more. After the game, Teague said, "We spent a lot of time practicing our defense. A lot of

time practicing our rotations and just competing at the highest level that we can compete in over practice. We've only had like three practices since the pause, so of course there was some slippage there, but I feel like we played pretty good defense today."

Drew also credited practice time. He added, "We worked on the defensive end, a lot of our defensive drills that we did in the non-conference, preseason, to get ready for play, and things that when you're playing games you can't do because you can't tire your guys out going into games. You're more worried about fresh legs, scouting opponents, making sure you're offensively, defensively, ready to execute, rather than just getting back to the basics of what our defense is about and just the basic closeouts and rotations and schemes. We were able to really get back to the basics and improve that and refresh their memory."

There was a real concern from many folks that Baylor would not get back to this level. Maybe one game isn't a sufficient sample, but the Bears seemed so much better in the season's most important game. Two weeks ago in Waco, the Bears just seemed a bit off. Guys would end up in the wrong spots. In Kansas City, other than Davion Mitchell, everyone seemed to end up in the wrong spot defensively or let the offensive player drive away from the help.

MaCio Teague celebrates after scoring during the first half against Hartford. Teague led Baylor in scoring with 22 points.

Today, the pick-and-roll defense stymied almost any advantage. I asked Drew about that, and he credited, "our hands were a lot more active. I thought we contested passes a lot better. Again, our rotations were earlier, crisper, we did a better job communicating who had what. I think a couple days of practices really translated." From across the court, Jonathan Tchamwa Tchatchoua shouted out pick-and-roll coverages. He shouted "ice" and "switch" at the right moment to force turnovers. In one key sequence he went in for a steal, which led to a dunk in transition.

The Bears were more than defense today. Adam Flagler had 12 points and Matt Mayer added eight. After an anemic showing in Kansas City, this was a real improvement. The Bears need that duo and Tchamwa Tchatchoua to provide scoring as the Bears advanced in this field.

MaCio Teague's also playing his best basketball. Once again he led Baylor in scoring with 22 points. Jared Butler added nine assists, as he eviscerated Hartford's planned pick-and-roll coverage. And Mitchell played such great defense that Hartford's player nearly broke his own ankles trying to evade the nation's premiere defender.

Nothing is guaranteed in March. Oral Roberts just upset Ohio State. Baylor built such a gargantuan second half lead that both fanbases booed when the game switched off the giant video board at Lucas Oil Stadium. When the announcer let the crowd know about the under eight media timeout, jubilation filled the arena as the spectators saw Ohio State's promising campaign end before the second day of the dance. ∎

Jonathan Tchamwa Tchatchoua puts pressure on Hartford's Miroslav Stafl. Baylor clicked defensively in the Round of 64, forcing 24 turnovers.

Baylor 76, Wisconsin 63
March 21, 2021 ▪ Indianapolis, Indiana

MAYER ANSWERS THE CALL

Bears Top Badgers to Advance to Sweet 16

After Loyola eviscerated No. 1 seed Illini earlier in the day, the Bears had to know nothing is guaranteed as a No. 1 seed in the NCAA Tournament. But behind a spectacular performance from Matthew Mayer, the Bears are headed to the Sweet 16 for the fifth time since 2010.

Jonathan Tchamwa Tchatchoua picked up two quick fouls. He added a third with 7:51 left. Those calls were tough for Baylor, but the officials called a tight game today. With Tchamwa Tchatchoua headed to the bench, the Bears inserted Mayer. Scott Drew said after, "Well, Matt was huge with Jon in foul trouble, and again, you've got to have depth and you've got to have multiple scorers." The Bears ended up getting stops on 6-of-7 possessions to end the half and thanks to a nice pass from Davion Mitchell to Adam Flagler, hit a buzzer beating three to lead by 13 at the half.

Mayer came alive offensively in the second half. He scored nine of his 17 points in the period. While Wisconsin made a run to pull within seven, Mayer hit a big three to eliminate the kind of pressure that makes one or two plays capable of ending the season.

Two other times when Wisconsin pulled within single digits, Mayer added a bucket. Wisconsin coach Greg Gard said, "But I even thought the difference today was Mayer, the plays he made off the bench. When they needed baskets in the second half, he answered for them."

Wisconsin elected to primarily play drop pick-and-roll coverage. I asked Mitchell about that alignment, and he said, "It was definitely similar to Illinois'. They dropped coverages, something that we love to see. We kind of got used to it. We used to do it in practice. We had to switch it up a little bit, so we just tried to take advantage of what the defense gave us, and we did great today." That coverage led to a bevy of Baylor buckets in the first half. In the second half, Wisconsin dropped again, and Mayer hit Mark Vital for a dunk. Wisconsin would never seriously threaten again.

Perhaps Mayer's most impressive skill in Hinkle was his defensive play in the second half. Wisconsin cut the lead to seven, and D'Mitrik Trice started hitting tough shots. The Bears had Mayer in, and he switched ball screens. That left him covering Wisconsin's senior guard. But he forced Trice into three tough jump shots. He missed all of them. Gard said, "The defensive pressure of Baylor. They went small and were switching everything and made it really hard to be able to get to where we wanted to get to. So that was — I'll give credit to

Baylor's Mark Vital celebrates after the Bears beat the Badgers 76-63 for a spot in the Sweet 16.

Baylor for getting us out of what we wanted to do."

The Badgers wanted to go big, but they couldn't stay that way. The Badgers had a size advantage, but with Mayer hanging out around the perimeter, Gard said, "When they came back with Mayer, it obviously made it a lot harder to do that."

Mayer finished with 17 points, six rebounds and two steals. Maybe the Bears still win without Mayer's performance. The strength of the 2021 Bears is that the team can survive rough stretches from key players. Davion Mitchell is a supreme defender. Jared Butler can run off eight points quickly and MaCio Teague has been Baylor's best scorer since the return. Someone from that trio is virtually guaranteed to have a big night, which means anyone else stepping up makes Baylor too tough to beat for even most teams in this tournament.

The Bears have depth that makes them nearly unstoppable. Wisconsin hit 8-of-17 threes before garbage time. Despite that hot shooting, Wisconsin never made it that close. The Badger faithful cheered loudly in the reduced capacity crowd. They couldn't will their team to a level Baylor hit, and Wisconsin can't.

With Tchamwa Tchatchoua rolling so well, Flagler back to what he was before the pause and Thamba providing some real moments now, the Bears are clearly back as the real challenger to Gonzaga's path to the first undefeated season since 1976. And if Mayer plays like he did this round, Baylor will win every round. ■

Matthew Mayer (24) blocks the shot of Wisconsin forward Micah Potter (11) during the first half. Mayer stepped up with 17 points, six rebounds and two steals.

11
FORWARD

MARK VITAL

Fifth-Year Senior Emerges as Leader for Baylor

March 25, 2021

When Baylor won its first conference championship since 1950 with a win over West Virginia, Scott Drew immediately jumped on Mark Vital's back. When I asked him about that after, he jokingly said, "He's the only one who's been here longer than me."

Over his years at Baylor, Vital's been quite the guy on and off the court. A defender capable of guarding all five positions, and a friend that prefers old school hits to the newest pump up music, Vital is a unique guy on the best Baylor team ever.

Thanks to a visit to Lake Charles, Louisiana, Vital ended up at Baylor. He says that Scott Drew arrived in his town and, "I'm just hoping my friends and guys around don't harm Coach Drew. I'm like, 'this is a bad neighborhood, why's he pulling up?' He'd call my dad and try and catch me to see what I'm doing. He just popped up. He was crazy. The thing going through my head is, 'why are you here?' He came in, 'Hey, it's the big dog.' He'd sit on the couch, make himself at home, go into the fridge. Coach Drew's crazy, man."

When Vital got to Waco, things weren't always easy. He says, "Growing up it was tough and hard. I had a couple friends that passed away. That kind of played a part in kind of my mental and never hit me. And me being away from home — when I had to go from Lake Charles to Dallas (for high school) — because I was away from my mom and had a lot of anxiety at the time. And then my freshman year was hard because I really wanted to play. And that brought on a lot of stuff."

During his freshman season, Vital redshirted. With Johnathan Motley and Ish Wainright set as forwards, Vital wasn't going to play much. That talented Baylor squad achieved the program's first ever No. 1 ranking. He says, "I wanted to play so bad, and it was crazy, bro."

Vital didn't get the help he needed immediately. But eventually he realized it was okay finally ask for help. He says his counselor "helped me understand you can get help and not feel like you're being judged. My thought was 'why am I going to talk to a counselor and get judged?' That was my thing. And at one point, the only way I was getting through

Mark Vital blocks a shot attempt by Oklahoma guard Elijah Harkless during the regular season. Vital verbally committed to Baylor following his freshman year of high school back in 2013. He leaves as one of the winningest players in program history.

it was getting my mind on different stuff. But for people that can't get access to that, they need to talk to someone."

He also recognized that there are unique ways to deal with the pain and struggles he faced. He says, "I have a pit. I used to talk to my dog. They just sit there and be cute, but you think they're listening. I talked to my dog a lot. And prayed a lot."

As a result of seeking out counseling and talking with others around him, Vital says, "Now that I've grieved, I'm happy to talk about that. I've dealt with a lot of depression and anxiety. Now I've battled depression and anxiety. I'm in a real great place."

As COVID-19 shut down the season, Vital had to decide whether to return to Baylor or try and play professional basketball. In his announcement video, he mentioned that he nearly went pro. But he says that after a tough loss to Kansas — which denied Baylor the 2019-2020 Big 12 title — "it really molded us to come back. We can't go out. We gotta come back and win. That's what we're doing. I said unfinished business earlier in the year." Davion Mitchell decided to forego the NBA Draft process, and both Jared Butler and MaCio Teague went through the process and reached the same conclusion as Vital: they'd come back to Baylor and try and win the conference title.

The summer wasn't easy on anyone. Vital says, "All right, so, I had one moment where I was like, 'Why did I come back?' I was more so thinking about the training. We couldn't really get into the gym. When we were in quarantine I had a gym I could go for lifting and everything. When I came back, I got to school, I hadn't touched weights in almost a month. Grocery stores were closed. It was just a weird time. I was thinking, 'I can't do it.' But I got used to it and got a routine. And as you see, now I don't regret it. I don't regret none of it."

Not being able to exercise is easy for most of us. It's probably easier than actually exercising. At Tuesday's press conference, Scott Drew offer his explanation for why coaches might have stopped wearing suits this year. "I think because of COVID. We all put on about 10 or 15 pounds, so we couldn't fit in our suits. We had to go to the polos." But for Vital, lifting weights is one of his favorite activities. Baylor's strength coach and director of athletic performance, Charlie Melton, tells me, "Mark's incredible. He could be a strength coach."

Although nobody on the 2020-2021 Bears ranked as a 5-star prospect, the Bears are immensely talented. Mitchell and Butler are definitely going to get drafted, and probably in the first round. Matthew Mayer might be a first-round pick in the 2022 NBA Draft; Vital's made the last two All-Big 12 defensive teams. And Teague has been of the country's best guards over the last few weeks.

With that cadre of players, Vital's emerged as a leader. Melton tells me, "Mark is really passionate, very protective of his crew and his people. He doesn't like to be challenged or embarrassed publicly and has come a long ways in terms of dealing with that. There's a song where they say, 'here comes the red again,' there's a saying, 'see through the red.' That's been a big talking point and seeing through the red, it's okay to be angry and aggressive. You can't lose your mind. He's really learned to channel that and not put himself (there) in turns of hurting the team. Early on he'd get mad at practice. Practice would stop….He's a leader, you lead in two ways. You either lead intentionally or unintentionally. A lot of times he'd lead unintentionally. Now he's learned to channel that and lead intentionally."

The Bears offense took off to begin the campaign. Baylor played Washington in its second game. The Huskies knocked off Baylor in that same game last season.

The Bears had an easier time dispatching this year's Huskies, winning 86-52. The Bears put Vital in the middle of Washington's 2-3 zone, and he finished with four assists. He says, "I'm a very underrated passer. I've always been a great passer. One of my favorite players is Magic Johnson. I'm an old school guy, so I watch a lot of film on him. I'm a very underrated passer. If you see some of the passes I do in practice, you'd probably think I'm an elite passer…me finding other guys is who I am. I have great vision. Some people see it, some don't. I've always been a good passer."

That's the issue with some analysis of Vital. His game doesn't light up the traditional box score. In the era of 3-point shooting, he doesn't take or make them in games. Some people think that means the Bears are better off playing someone else that can space the floor.

The problem with some people is that they're wrong. Against Illinois, Jared Butler got into the lane and threw up a lob for Jonathan Tchamwa Tchatchoua. The Illini big man shouted, "flare screen" as Vital prepared to set a screen for Teague. It turned out the defending big man ended up so terrified of Vital setting that screen to free up Teague that he recovered late and fouled Tchamwa Tchatchoua. In a quick live view, it seems like Butler and Tchamwa Tchatchoua drew the foul. But without Vital capturing the big's attention, Butler and Tchamwa Tchatchoua have to overwhelm a focused big man. Those small sequences from Vital—a screen here or notching one more offensive rebound—provide key opportunities. And for a Baylor team that seems to just knock folks out, keeping it close is often all that's necessary for the country's top 3-point shooting team to eventually blow teams away.

Not everyone would embrace that role: the idea that your job is to screen for someone and not be the 20 point a night player. Presented with a role like Vital's, some might transfer. Others might decide to go pro. Maybe they'd be justified thinking they could be a major scorer somewhere else.

But Vital understands what makes him a special player, and he tries to maximize those skills. He says, "My thing is like, I watch a lot of Draymond (Green), Dennis Rodman, PJ Tucker at one point, Tony Allen. So I watched all those guys. I gotta do what I can. They sagged off them. If I was on a different team, where a coach said, 'I need you to shoot threes or get 20 or 30 a game,' I would change my mind and be an elite scorer. In high school I was like that. But I changed my role when Coach Drew asked. For one, when you step back, you give me a rest on defense. Second, if you wait in the paint, I can set a flare (screen), and Jared is going to hit a three and (the opposing) coach will get mad. Then I'm fast enough, I'll drive around. A lot of guys know me from high school because I've been in college for five years, so they're trying to step up."

The Bears went on a COVID-19 pause for 21 days. After starting undefeated, Baylor trailed Iowa State — a team that finished winless in the Big 12 and ended up firing Steve Prohm — by 15 points. Vital says, "We had that long pause. It was probably the worst thing ever. Everyone was back to square one. Guys were out of shape. Dribbling ball at home. (We were) on Zoom. When we got back that first game we saw we were struggling with Iowa State, we were like, 'we gotta pick it up.'"

As the Iowa State game neared its end, Vital met the moment. Rasir Bolton had a path to the hoop, and Vital reached up and swatted the ball. He says, "My mindset is like a lot of guys do a good job setting up for me. They know I'm super athletic, so they try to go under or make someone make a dumb shot and clean it up. Me and Davion do a good job. I can run into someone and make them change their shot up. We get that from LeBron and Dwyane Wade. They did that a lot."

The Bears' undefeated season ended in their next game against Kansas. After the game, Vital didn't get too down. He says, "We knew that game was going to be tough because it was their senior night. And it was going to be physical and everything like that. At the same time, we knew we were coming back from that and (they'd) take advantage of that because Bill Self is a great coach and he knows if you're coming from a pause, you're not in shape like you were. Those guys were running it down our throat and going and going and going. We lost a game. Of course we were really pissed because we really wanted it. We had a goal to still win the conference and take the next few games. We got on the bus and everyone was mad, and we talked about it."

Vital's focused on winning a national title. In a controlled environment—or whatever euphemism the NCAA promulgates instead of just saying "bubble"—Vital describes the team's activities. He says, "What's so beneficial about being in the bubble, they give us all healthy foods so I have no choice. Don't get me wrong, I had a couple nights where I ordered DoorDash, but those prices hit me. The check was $30; it's not worth it, bro, so I might as well eat the grilled cheese downstairs." Vital did not elect to get the Nashville hot chicken grilled cheese, featuring macaroni on the sandwich, down the street from his hotel. That was probably a wise move because that meal in downtown Indianapolis caused such pronounced stomach pain for two Baylor media members that they worried they'd miss the game. Both of us made the game, but I still feel so ashamed that I ate that sandwich that it felt better leaving some ambiguity in the original sentence.

Vital is good friends with Baylor basketball graduate assistant Chris Nottingham. He's been with the team for years as both a manager and graduate assistant. He tells me that back in 2018 he took over helping with the uniforms. He reminisces, "We had just played SFA and lost at the buzzer, obviously. I knew Mark had a bit of a temper, and I knew not to test him he got mad. When he walked off the court, I could tell he was angry, and his hands were on the neckline of his jersey, I was like, 'God, please, don't you do it.' He didn't look up and just shredded the jersey right down the middle. We didn't wear white for a month because we had to get one express shipped to us."

Not long after the pair developed a close friendship. Nottingham says, "If you'd have told me Mark would have been one of my best friends in three of four years, I would have thought you were nuts."

The two became such good friends that Vital got worried when Nottingham didn't answer his phone when the two had dinner plans. Nottingham fell asleep on his couch, and with his roommates out of town, nobody woke him up to meet Vital. He says, "I woke up to this dude picking me (up). Mark got into my house and picked me up and carried me out to eat. I'm not huge. I'm not small. I've never felt so small to be picked up. That was the freakiest way to be waken up ever."

When I asked Nottingham how Vital got into his house, he says, "He never told me. I went to sleep and thought about it every night....my roommates weren't home. I just don't really try to think too much into it when it comes to Mark. He's a resourceful individual."

That resourcefulness has meant helping out others. Melton recounts, "On Baylor's campus they have a campus Farmer's Market, and they can get fruits and vegetables and load them up to their dorms. Twice Mark comes in carrying a big box, and it's a big box of dried goods and watermelon because he knows my kids like watermelon and he said, 'I

Mark Vital dunks against Wisconsin during the Bears' second-round win over the Badgers.

picked up watermelon for you kids.' He has such a big heart and people don't realize that when he's the villain or he's mister 95 and does the dirty work."

Vital oscillates between being the funny guy that can be serious and the serious guy that can be funny. Over the summer, Baylor's players and staff had numerous discussions about race. Those conversations were often difficult, but they felt productive to many of the players and staff.

Nottingham says that during one meeting, "Mark was kind of quiet the whole time, then he spoke up…it's the most serious mood in this room,

and everyone's willing their heart out. Mark got on this tangent, 'some of my best friends in this room are white,' he's listing off white people, then he says, 'Chris, I don't even know what you are." Nottingham said he joined the whole room in laughing hysterically as everyone came together.

In two months, Vital will walk across the Ferrell Center stage and accept his degree. He'll be the first person in his family to graduate from college. He explains, "I got something that I can change and fall back on. That's going to change a lot. And my kids, that's going to be different." ■

Baylor 62, Villanova 51
March 27, 2021 ▪ **Indianapolis, Indiana**

AN ELITE SECOND HALF

Defense Steps Up as Baylor Overcomes Seven-Point Halftime Deficit

Despite trailing 30-23 at halftime, and shooting 3-of-19 from three, Baylor played pristine second half basketball to beat Villanova 62-51.

The first half set up the recipe to beat Baylor. The Bears started 2-of-12 from deep. Jared Butler, a unanimous All-American, started 2-of-8 from the field. Villanova began 3-of-7 from deep. Jeremiah Robinson Earl and Jermaine Samuels seemed too good inside, combining for 15 first half points. Although Baylor pressured Villanova's guards, the Wildcats still got inside.

In the second half, Baylor started to get inside on offense. After going 4-of-9 near the rim in the first half — and with Villanova's imposing frontline making shots tough near the rim — I didn't think Baylor could work scoring inside. That's why I am not coaching an Elite Eight team, and Scott Drew and his staff are.

After the game, Drew said, "When we were 2-for-12 at the half we knew we had to get inside. We had decent looks, not great looks. Credit Villanova for doing a great job contesting shots. I thought our guards did a great job not settling and probing more. And because of that we shot 53 percent second half."

Davion Mitchell and Adam Flagler combined for 21 points in the half. Flagler hit one three to finish with 16 points. Otherwise, every point from the pair happened inside the arc. Mark Vital made a tough layup. Jared Butler put Villanova in a spin cycle for a layup too. And MaCio Teague used his superb footwork to add another.

Perhaps the defense being this good again is the main takeaway. Yes, Villanova missed a few open triples. The Wildcats finished the half 0-of-7 from deep. But even conceding that, Baylor still held Villanova to .7 points per possession that half. The nation's worst offense averages .86 points per possession, which makes that mark incredible.

The defense being this good makes Baylor a champion team. In the seven games Baylor played to end the season—after returning from the 21-day COVID layoff—Baylor gave up at least one adjusted point per possession. In every game in the NCAA Tournament, Baylor's held the opponent to fewer than one adjusted point per possession. Winning a championship normally requires ranking in the top 20 in adjusted offensive and defensive efficiency. The Bears have been a top 20 offense all season. They've played as a top 20 defense against during the tournament, as they had before the pause.

The Bear's defense appears back because the team plays the same style, regardless of opponent. The Bears make some adjustments, but the formula is constant: Baylor pressures guards with Mitchell. Villanova had six turnovers in each of its last two games. It had nine in the second half.

Baylor's Adam Flagler waves to fans after beating Villanova 62-51 in the Sweet 16. Flagler put up a team-high 16 points.

Villanova forward Jermaine Samuels, center, tries to pass while under pressure from Baylor's Adam Flagler and Flo Thamba.

Mitchell is the country's best defender. He won Big 12 Defensive Player of the Year, and forced two big turnovers in the second half. Life is different driving against Mitchell, and it ended the hope of Villanova making an Elite Eight.

After the game, Mitchell noted, "We knew if we wanted to win we had to turn them over. We had to make them feel uncomfortable. They're a really fundamental team. They don't turn the ball over. They're number one in the country in not to turning the ball over. For us to win, we had to get them out of their comfort zone, and I think we did a really good job of that."

On top of a great defensive performance, the Bears' bench is back. Jonathan Tchamwa Tchatchoua did a nice job on Jeremiah Robinson-Earl in the first half. He left in the second half after making a scouting error that led to a dunk, but Matthew Mayer had a nice game as well, providing quality defense and some timely rebounds. When Villanova got Baylor into the bonus, Flagler put them away hitting all six free throw attempts.

Baylor's been to the Elite Eight twice before under Drew. The difference this time is that Baylor will be favored against Arkansas or Oral Roberts. While both teams are good—and Oral Roberts is playing at a whole new level compared to earlier in the season—2012 Kentucky with Anthony Davis does not loom.

Perhaps most importantly, the best Baylor team ever will take the floor on Monday. If you'd told me before this game that Baylor would shoot this poorly and get a combined 14 points from Butler and Teague, I'd have thought it was a heartbreaking end to Baylor's season.

But the Bears are simply too good. They've done everything for two years to put themselves in position to make the program's first Final Four since 1950. And with what Baylor's shown in this tournament, they should be heavily favored to make it there. ■

The Baylor Bears qualified for their third Elite Eight appearance under head coach Scott Drew.

Baylor 81, Arkansas 72
March 29, 2021 ▪ Indianapolis, Indiana

THE FINAL WEEKEND AWAITS

Bears top Razorbacks to Reach first Final Four since 1950

As Baylor's players grabbed and threw green and yellow confetti into the air, the celebration reached its apex. What once seemed unthinkable became reality as Monday became Tuesday in Indianapolis: Baylor basketball is going to the Final Four. The Bears are headed there for the first time since 1950.

Baylor was easily one of the country's top two teams from the beginning of the season through a double-digit victory over Texas in Austin. Then COVID-19 struck over half the players, forcing a 21-day pause. The Bears finished the regular season 5-2 and Big 12 Champions. Though Baylor wasn't quite the same during that stretch.

Once they returned, the Bears weren't the same on defense. Head coach Scott Drew said afterwards that, "you see your defense go from one to three to five to 12 to 20 and eventually got to 44. And once we lost to Oklahoma State, I believe in that game we only got two or three stops in the last eight minutes of the game." Just isolating that seven-game stretch, per Torvik, Baylor ranked 190th in adjusted defensive efficiency. Baylor knew it had to improve on that.

In the first half against Arkansas, Baylor tested that proposition while the offense seemed capable of carrying whatever the defense provided. For 12 minutes, Baylor scored over two points per possession. Arkansas would have been better off surrendering dunks. The Razorbacks did that plenty of times. Jonathan Tchamwa Tchatchoua and Matthew Mayer slammed it down. The Razorbacks faced the impossible task of defending a Baylor offense with more weapons than NATO.

The Razorbacks answered, though. Davion Mitchell, the South Region's most outstanding player, picked up his third foul in the first half. He finished the half at +16, but Arkansas cut the deficit to eight at the break.

Eventually everyone starts missing shots. Baylor ranks as the country's top 3-point shooting team. Yet that didn't mean Baylor would make everything. The Bears started struggling from the field and Arkansas pulled within four with 6:50 left. It felt like maybe the Muss Bus had a little more fuel to get Arkansas past Baylor. The ghost of Baylor not holding a five-point second half lead against Duke in the 2010 Elite Eight loomed.

Then Baylor turned it up defensively. Baylor held Hartford to a catastrophic .71 adjusted points per possession in Lucas Oil Stadium to open this tournament. It then held Wisconsin and Villanova

MaCio Teague defends against Arkansas guard JD Notae. Baylor's defense came alive in the second half, limiting the No. 3 seed Razorbacks to one point per possession.

below one point per possession. That same defense emerged in the second half. Arkansas scored just one point per possession in the second half.

Jonathan Tchamwa Tchatchoua, a man that didn't score five points a game as a freshman at UNLV, drew a charge and blocked a shot. The Bears held Arkansas to one point for the next four minutes.

Offense remains necessary to win championships, and MaCio Teague provided it. Despite starting 0-of-4 from three, Teague swished two triples with Arkansas down six points with six minutes remaining.

Multiple people inside the program raved about Teague's work to perfect his shooting motion over the last few months, and it paid off in the biggest moment of Baylor's season. Suddenly Arkansas found themselves trailing by 11. They'd never threaten again.

I asked Teague about those two threes after the game. He said, "You know, my teammates there they kept finding me. I think two possessions before that, Jared, he drove baseline, looked to (indiscernible) and looked to me in the corner — looked the opposing player off and threw it to me in the corner. And I shot it and I missed it. When I was running down the floor, I remember my teammate saying "good shot" — I can't remember who it was who said, 'good shot, shoot it again.' So I got another opportunity, they found me, and I hit it. And I saw, when Davion drove, I saw him look at me before he drove, to see where the defense was going to be. And he found me and I knocked another one down. So the credit goes to those guys for keeping faith in me."

Baylor wouldn't have won this game without every player in the rotation. Adam Flagler notched four steals. When Baylor seemed incapable of slowing down Arkansas, Flagler stepped in to give

Jared Butler ascends to the hoop while guarded by Arkansas defenders Jaylin Williams and Jalen Tate.

Baylor transition chances. A former Presbyterian player, he might be the best player on next year's Baylor team. But he was pretty special tonight, adding 10 points and a final three that left Arkansas not even attempting to foul late.

The list of big moments from everyone in the rotation could stretch on. When Mitchell picked up his third foul in the first half, Jared Butler steadied the offense, scoring 11 first half points. Mark Vital had a tip-in dunk late that stopped an Arkansas run, and Flo Thamba hit a pair of shots near the rim before the shot clock expired.

Mitchell proved too much offensively in the second half. He finished with 10 points in the period, as Baylor worked to force an Arkansas big man to guard him. Regardless of defender, he found his way to the hoop.

Mitchell moves left faster than a Democratic candidate in a Vermont primary. Or as Jalen Tate said after the contest, "That Davion Mitchell is one of the fastest guys I've ever guarded, especially this year. He's a tough cover. You could tell they're a completely different team on both sides of the ball. He's a facilitator for them as well as just their anchor defensively."

Baylor certainly has the best team in program history. But in this single elimination format, nothing is guaranteed. The Elite Eight has been the graveyard of national championship caliber teams, perhaps most recently exemplified by Zion Williamson's Duke team. Tonight Baylor had every answer.

This is also a testament to the program and culture built by Scott Drew. He took over a program so devastated by scandal that the NCAA precluded non-conference games in his third season. Baylor's history from 1951 to Drew taking over was a 1988 NCAA Tournament berth. To go

from a history so scant to one that features an outright Big 12 title—despite playing five fewer games than some Big 12 teams—and a Final Four, is nothing short of miraculous.

When Drew was asked if he ever had second thoughts about coming here, he said, "No, I prayed about it. I felt led to come here. I really believed in the vision of the school, from the president and the administrators during that time and what they wanted Baylor to continue to grow and become."

The Bears are made up of under-recruited men and transfers. None ranked in the top 50 nationally. Teague, tonight's leading scorer, started at UNC-Asheville because nobody thought he could play at a power six school. Mitchell rode the bench as a freshman at Auburn and looked for a new start in Waco. He will likely be a lottery pick in the NBA Draft. Butler went from outside the top 75 as a recruit to the first unanimous All-American at Baylor.

Unselfishness describes this program. As he basked in the victory, Teague noted, "It means a tremendous amount to me but even more to the program. No person is bigger than the program. What we did was history here. Really happy for Coach Drew. He's been here for 18 years."

The Bears have achieved so much already. Four of these starters played on last year's team that won 23 consecutive games—the longest streak ever for a Big 12 team.

The Bears don't need much of a winning streak now. Two more wins and Baylor wins the national title. ■

Davion Mitchell drives on Arkansas forward Justin Smith en route to 10 second-half points.

ACKNOWLEDGMENTS

This book and journey wouldn't have been possible without the help and time from so many people that didn't need to give it.

Thank you to David Kaye. He's Baylor's SID and is one of America's best people. He helped me schedule interviews, and whenever I'd ask for one more person to interview, he'd come through. None of this would be possible without him.

Thank you to Scott Drew, Jerome Tang, John Jakus and Al Brooks III. Baylor's coaching staff answered some of my goofiest questions and always helped showcase their players.

I'm grateful to Baylor's graduate assistants. Rem Bakamus provided excellent story ideas and connected me with folks. Matt Gray, Obim Okeke, Chris Nottingham and Jake McGee gave me unique stories and let me have all the time I needed.

Charlie Melton gave me great information for a profile. He did that without almost zero notice.

This book is about the players, and they all gave me more time than I deserved. Jared Butler shouting "Kendall" at press conferences and talking to me over the last three years has been one of the highlights of my life. Davion Mitchell broke down plays with me during Baylor's COVID pause and when I'd ask a weird question, he'd always engage. MaCio Teague and I had a great chat over the summer about his journey and basketball. Matthew Mayer opened up about mental health in a way I'm super grateful for. Jonathan Tchamwa Tchatchoua helped me learn about Cameroon and what it's like to dunk. Mark Vital spent an hour talking with me during the NCAA Tournament and went in-depth about mental health and the full journey. Freddie Gillespie, Tristan Clark, Jake Lindsey and King McClure also let me write longform articles over the last few years. That made this book better than it would have without them.

Thank you to the Johnson County District Attorney's Office. Andrew Jennings, Marissa Bell, Xavier Andrews, Melinda Parrish, Whitney Meador, Ann Henderson, Nick Zych, Vanessa Riebli, Brenna Lynch, Letitia Ferwalt, Beth Morris, David Greenwald, Jonathan Zadina, Samantha Shannon, Tyler Childress, Alex Scott, Megan Sachse, Chris McMullin, Steve Howe and so many others didn't complain if I'd ask to move lunch around or have assistance to make sure I could both cover this team and prosecute folks. They also found it okay that I went back-and-forth between Waco and Indianapolis over the last few months.

Thank you to my great friends for their support (many of you are listed above). Brian Box, Josh DeMoss, Aaron Vanderpool, Trent Rogers, Jono Guevara, Shakey Strickland, and Sam and Colleen Hogan.

Thank you to members of Baylor media for being a sounding board. Many of you are also great friends. Ashley Hodge, John Werner, Mark Seymour, Peter Pope, David Hornbeak, David Fankhauser, Matt Wilson, Dex Hinton, Amy Paggit, Fielding Montgomoery, Colt Barber, David Smoak, Paul Catalina, Jason King, Kurtis Quillin and many others. I'd put Baylor media up with any team.

Finally, I want to thank my family. My mom and dad never told me to stop trying to cover basketball. They've been the foundation of support that made everything possible. I am the luckiest person in the world that I got them as parents. My sister, Allison, brother-in-law, Aaron, niece Avery, and nephew, Cooper, are an amazing family that provides crucial support. I'm blessed to have all of them in my life. And thank you to my Aunt Connie, Uncle Gary and cousins Jeremy and Aimee for the hospitality in Indianapolis. As well as my Aunt and Uncle Doug and Marissa Kaut for their support over the years. ∎